BABY
NAMES
2011

Eleanor Turner

white
LADDER

Acknowledgements

I would like to extend my utmost gratitude to Cerys Owen, Shelley Heck, Michael Turner and Robin Boothroyd for their contributions; without them this book would have been much shorter. My thanks are also given to Holly Ivins at Crimson Publishing for her patience and guidance throughout the project. Finally, the greatest thanks go to Owen Henri Turner, who grew patiently inside me while I wrote this book and waited to be born until I had chosen his name.

This edition first published in Great Britain 2010 by
Crimson Publishing, a division of Crimson Business Ltd
Westminster House
Kew Road
Richmond
Surrey
TW9 2ND

© Crimson Publishing, 2010

A catalogue record for this book is available from the British Library.

ISBN 978 1 90541 068 2

Contents

A note on how to use this book

While the author and publisher acknowledge that names may vary widely on spellings and pronunciations, names have been arranged by common spellings and first initial only. Alternative first initial spellings are listed under their relative letter, but spelling variations with the same first initial are listed only once, under the most common spelling.

Introduction

 Words have meaning and names have power.

Anonymous

Picking a name for your baby is one of the most enjoyable rites of passage for a new parent. It's also one of the most daunting. A name *is* important because it is the one thing to stay with your child throughout their entire life and affects who it is they become. Having a name which they can live with and be proud of, therefore, is crucial to having a good start in life and this book will show you exactly how to pick the right one.

Sometimes choosing the right name is simply a case of hearing one you like near the birth of your baby and knowing instantly that you've chosen correctly. However, for the vast majority of parents the naming process becomes a complex minefield of trying to please parents, grandparents, friends and siblings while trying to avoid embarrassing acronyms with their newborn's initials, or names that could be shortened into ridiculous nicknames. Parents also like to choose something unique, but not *too* unique, or common but not *too* common, or a name which is symbolic of a cultural event at the time of the baby's birth. A name could come from an admired celebrity's baby, a sports star, or an influential historical or political figure. It could also come from the family tree, or be part of a long-standing tradition where sons are named after fathers and daughters are named after mothers. The possibilities and chances to make a mistake or offend someone are practically endless and it's understandable that it can send some parents into panic mode.

Well, never fear. This book talks you through each of your options carefully and discusses how to solve your baby-naming dilemmas in practical ways. It's also updated annually, which means you'll know the latest trends in baby names and find out the most popular names for your baby's classmates to help guide you towards your final decision. If you are a parent for whom finding your baby's name is simply a case of seeing it written down, then you'll love the dozens of lists we've included, highlighting the popular, the classic and the downright weird names children have been given over the years.

The average length of a baby name is six letters.

This book is broken into two sections: the first deals with how to figure out what to name your child through a series of questions and suggestions, and the second gives you a meaning for each name you're considering using. There's no right or wrong way to use this book, just as there's no right or wrong way to make your baby-naming decision, so dip in, find some names you like and use the suggestions we've given you to work out if one of them is a winner!

part one

1

What was hot in 2010?

❝A good name is rather to be chosen than great riches.

Proverbs XXII, verse 1 ❞

2010 top 10 baby boy names

1. Jack
2. Harry
3. Alfie
4. Thomas
5. Oliver
6. Daniel
7. Joshua
8. Charlie
9. Mohammed
10. George

2010 top 10 baby girl names

1.	Olivia	6.	Jessica
2.	Ruby	7.	Amelia
3.	Emily	8.	Chloe
4.	Grace	9.	Isabella
5.	Lily	10.	Emma

The rise of quirky names continues…

Since 2008 an interesting phenomenon has taken place: only 50% of babies born in the UK have had their names represented in the Top 50 of recorded births. The remaining 50% have all had such unique and diverse names that they do not get placed high enough in the charts to be listed. Although this has been the first time such a large number of names have not been represented, it has been a growing trend since the early 1980s. One possible explanation for this is that those children born since the early 1980s are now themselves having children. It seems likely that a parent with a slightly unusual name will feel more confident about giving their offspring a unique name if they have enjoyed their own growing up.

Some of Britain's quirky baby names during the last year have included Paprica, Caramel and Skylark for a girl, and Rocky, Rivers and Red for boys.

2010 popular boy name newcomers

- Archie
- Caleb
- Jacob
- Joel
- Lucas
- Sebastian
- Mohammed

2010 popular girl name newcomers

- Isabella
- Layla
- Lexi
- Lola
- Maisie
- Miley
- Sienna

...But traditional names also continue to impress

2010 also saw a continuation of the revival of previously outdated names. Names such as Alfie, Harry, Amelia and Ruby had dropped out of mainstream use by the 1960s and became vastly unpopular, but in the last five years names ending in –ie and –y have started to see a resurgence.

2010 was no different, with the Top 10 in both boys and girls names remaining largely unchanged. The reason for the resurgence of traditional names could be down to what is known as the '100-year rule.' In short, names that were popular 100 years ago are now being chosen again. Names associated with the great-grandfathers and great-

great-grandfathers of recent parents, such as Archie and Rose, are making a comeback. Perhaps this is because the current generations either want to connect with their family history or don't associate the names with a generation they remember.

Popular names of English and Scottish Kings and consorts for boys and girls

Alexander	Anna
Charles	Anne
Edward	Catherine
George	Eleanor
Henry	Elizabeth
James	Mairi
Richard	Margaret
Robert	Mary
Stephen	Matilda
William	Victoria

Popular choices remain popular

Other than two new entries in each list this year, the Top 10 for both boys and girls has contained the same names for the last four years. It seems then that although some parents like to be adventurous in their choice of name many pick a name for their child which doesn't have any quirky or unusual connotations, avoiding any possible assumptions people may make about an unusual name. However, the seemingly endless popularity of names like Jack may soon lead to a backlash against such overly chosen names.

Incredibly, Jack has remained the top choice for parents of newborn baby boys for 16 years in a row.

2

What does 2011 hold for baby names?

Will these trends continue?

Looking forward to 2011, the trend for choosing old fashioned or very unique names for babies seems set to continue. The Top 10 names will probably go largely unchanged for both boys and girls, but there may be a rise in the percentage of unique names not to make the Top 50. Paradoxically, there may also be a backlash against very popular names, as parents opt to not give their child the same name as four or five of their potential school friends.

As parents grow more globally aware and the demographics of the UK change, we may see more culturally and ethnically diverse names appearing in these lists, such as Ahmed, Aisha, Fatima and Tariq. This has already started to happen with the name Mohammed, the traditional choice for baby boys in Muslim families, which has now become so popular a choice in the UK that it entered the Top 10 for the first time last year.

Parents may also start looking further back into their family trees for inspiration, giving rise to many more African (Asante, Femi), Asian (Pang, Kaemon) and Middle English (Avery, Tate) names.

Finally, it seems likely that parents will continue the recent trend of naming their children shortened versions of longer, more traditional names. The name Maisie, for example, is a shortened version of Margaret, while Bobby is more usually written as Robert. The cult of celebrity and TV characters may be responsible for this, as viewers become more familiar with nicknames than actual names.

Predicted 2011 Top 10 baby boy names

1. Jack
2. Oliver
3. Thomas
4. Charlie
5. Harry

6. Alfie
7. Joshua
8. Daniel
9. George
10. Mohammed

Predicted 2011 Top 10 baby girl names

1. Ruby
2. Grace
3. Lily
4. Ella
5. Olivia

6. Emily
7. Amelia
8. Sophie
9. Chloe
10. Emma

2011 events

Other influences on the names parents choose in 2011 will come from the worlds of celebrity, politics and sport.

After the wealth of sporting events in 2010, 2011 seems tame in comparison. Although it may be the year of the IVth Commonwealth Youth Games (held this time on the Isle of Man), it seems unlikely that this event will be high-profile enough to effect any real change in baby name trends. However, after the Olympic Winter Games and the FIFA World Cup in 2010, a knock-on effect may still be occurring. Gold medallist Amy Williams could continue to see her name rise in popularity, as could the entire English or USA football teams.

The 2010 general election saw David Cameron assume the role of Prime Minister, which may lead to a surge in popularity of the name David in 2011 – it was last seen in 64th place in 2008. However, having a new Prime Minister does not always dictate an increase in babies born with the same name: the name Gordon did not push its way back into the UK's Top 100 after Gordon Brown took office in 2007 and Anthony also failed to remain popular during Tony Blair's time as PM; it was last seen in position number 98 in 2003 but has since dropped to 127 in recent years.

Interestingly, there is a trend of naming babies after the *children* of politicians – Barack Obama's daughters are named Malia and Sasha, and a variation of both of these entered the Top 100 names for girls in 2009. Perhaps David Cameron or Nick Clegg's childrens' names will also show a rise in popularity in 2011.

Also held in 2010 was the US Census, the results of which potentially determined the choices new parents made last year for their baby names. Although US data does not always correspond to UK data, the statistics have been of definite interest to name historians on both sides of the pond, particularly those awaiting the results of the 2011 UK Census.

The cult of celebrity

As always, the world of celebrities will continue to dominate choices made by parents, for better or worse.

Celebrities expecting babies in late 2010 and 2011 include Jamie and Jools Oliver (their fourth), and Alicia Keys (her first). If the choices of names these celebrities make are particularly noteworthy, they may well influence the choices made by the general population. The name Honor, for example, increased in popularity after the birth of Jessica

Alba's baby girl in 2008, as well as the name Ava, which has even jumped in popularity with celebrities themselves. Reese Witherspoon has been given credit for this surge: she called her daughter Ava, after actress Ava Gardner, in 1999 and the name jumped from rank number 259 to number 9 in 2005 and has stayed in the top five ever since.

In fact, after Britney Spears named her second son Jayden James in 2006, the name became the second most popular name for baby boys in New York City. Likewise, bad choices of names leave potential parents sniggering rather than considering, such as with the case of Amadeus Benedict Edley Luis, Boris Becker and Sharlely Kerssenberg's new son or Bodhi Hawn, Goldie Hawn's latest grandchild.

Celebrity baby boys of 2009/2010

Coleen and Wayne Rooney	Kai Wayne
Nicole Richie and Joel Madden	Sparrow James Midnight
Gisele Bündchen and Tom Brady	Benjamin Rein
Boris Becker and Sharlely Kerssenberg	Amadeus Benedict Edley Luis
Oliver Hudson and Erinn Bartlett	Bodhi Hawn
Jenna and Bodhi Elfman	Easton Quinn Monroe
Nicola McLean and Tom Williams	Striker
Sandra Bullock	Louis
Will and Viveca Ferrel	Axel
Jessica Taylor and Kevin Pietersen	Dylan

Celebrity baby girls of 2009/2010

Sarah Michelle Gellar and Freddie Prinze Jr.	Charlotte Grace
Ioan Gruffudd and Alice Evans	Ella Betsi Janet
Heidi Klum and Seal	Lou Solula
Matthew McConaughey and Camilla Alves	Vida
Joseph Fiennes and Maria Dolores Dieguez	Nicknamed 'Baby Love'
Joe and Carly Cole	Ruby Tatiana
Sara Cox and Ben Cyzer	Renee
Denise Van Outen and Lee Mead	Betsy
Jenny Platt and Rupert Hill	Matilda
Amanda Peet and David Benioff	Molly June
Mel Gibson and Oksana Grigorieva	Lucia Anne
Claudia Schiffer and Matthew Vaughn	Cosima Violet
Amy Adams and Darren Le Gallo	Aviana Olea
Kevin Costner and Christine Baumgartner	Grave Avery

Expected new arrivals in 2010/2011

Dannii Minogue and Kris Smith	(July 2010)
Danielle Lloyd and Jamie O'Hara	(July 2010)
Chanelle Hayes	(August 2010)
Jessica Taylor and Kevin Pietersen	(Summer 2010)
Jamie and Jools Oliver	(September 2010)
Sam Taylor-Wood and Aaron Johnson	(September 2010)
Lance Armstrong and Anna Hansen	(October 2010)
Matt and Luciana Damon	(Autumn 2010)
Mario Lopez and Courtney Mazza	(Autumn 2010)
Anne-Marie Duff and James McAvoy	(Unknown 2010)
Amy Poehler and Will Arnett	(Unknown 2010)
Isla Fisher and Sacha Baron Cohen	(Unknown 2010)
Alicia Keys and Swiss Beatz	(Unknown)
Celine Dion and Rene Angeli	(Unknown)
Rachel Stevens and Alex Bourne	(Unknown)

Unusual celebrity baby names of recent years

Amadeus (Boris Becker)

Apple (Gwyneth Paltrow and Chris Martin)

Blue Angel (U2's The Edge and Aislinn O'Sullivan)

Bluebell Madonna (Geri Halliwell)

Bodhi Hawn (Oliver Hudson and Erinn Bartlett)

Bronx Mowgli (Ashlee Simpson and Pete Wentz)

Brooklyn (David and Victoria Beckham – also parents to Romeo and Cruz)

Dixie Dot (Anna Ryder Richardson)

Ikhyd (M.I.A and Benjamin Brewer)

Kal-El Coppola (Nicholas Cage – Kal-El is Superman's original birth name)

Luna Coco Patricia (Frank Lampard and Elen Rives)

Petal Blossom Rainbow (Jules and Jamie Oliver – also parents to Daisy Boo and Poppy Honey)

Princess Tiaamii (Jordan and Peter Andre)

Shiloh Nouvel (Brad Pitt and Angelina Jolie)

Sparrow (Nicole Richie)

Sunday Rose (Nicole Kidman and Keith Urban)

Suri (Tom Cruise and Katie Holmes)

Kai Wayne (Wayne and Coleen Rooney)

Zuma Nesta Rock (Gwen Stefani and Gavin Rossdale)

2011 anniversaries

Significant anniversaries can potentially influence baby names.

In 2011 this includes the 2,500th anniversary (est.) of the Marathon, the 100th anniversary of the first car rally at Monte Carlo, the 100th anniversary of International Women's Day, the 50th anniversary of The Beatles' first performance, and 50 years since the birth of Diana, Princess of Wales. It will also be Barack Obama's 50th birthday and 25 years since the disaster at Chernobyl.

Don't be surprised, therefore, if the names Monte, Carlo, George, Paul, Ringo, John, Diana, Barack and even some Ukrainian names all jump in popularity. The very fact these names will be bandied around by the media will mean parents will start to consider them as potential candidates, even if they would never have considered them previously.

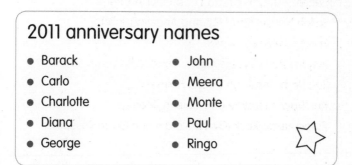

2011 anniversary names

- Barack
- Carlo
- Charlotte
- Diana
- George
- John
- Meera
- Monte
- Paul
- Ringo

3

How to choose a name

Top tips on choosing a name

- **Fall in love with the name(s) you've chosen.** If you plough through hundreds of names in this book and none of them jump off the page at you, then you probably haven't found the right one yet. Likewise, if a relative, friend, or even your spouse suggests a name and you wrinkle your nose every time you hear it, it's not the name for your baby.

- **Don't listen to other people.** Sometimes, grandparents and friends will offer 'advice' which may not always be welcome. It's also worth bearing in mind that if you've fallen in love with a name and it's either slightly unusual or doesn't follow the set pattern your partner's family have used for the last 50 years, sharing your choice of name with other people can lead them to criticise it, which you'd probably rather not hear if you've got your heart set on it. Also, if you're dispensing with tradition and don't plan on calling your newborn after their great-great-great-grandfather, keeping it a secret until after the birth and registration can work to your advantage. Trust your own instincts and remember: no-one will really care once they see your baby. Its name will simply be its name.

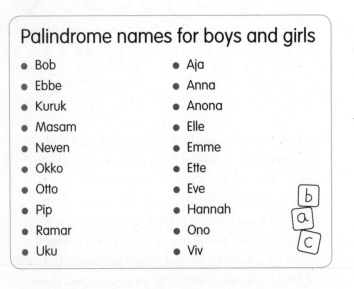

Palindrome names for boys and girls

- Bob
- Ebbe
- Kuruk
- Masam
- Neven
- Okko
- Otto
- Pip
- Ramar
- Uku
- Aja
- Anna
- Anona
- Elle
- Emme
- Ette
- Eve
- Hannah
- Ono
- Viv

- **Research.** You've already started the process of researching which name to pick simply by buying this book, but there are ways to expand the process if you wish to. The internet can be a fantastic way to look up meanings in more depth, or to find out if your baby's name is becoming more or less popular through the years. This is particularly useful if you want to avoid a situation where your daughter has the same name as three other children in her class, or if you don't want your son to be teased because his name sounds rude in another language. Other ways to do research include making lists of names you hear during the run-up to the birth, going back into history to find names of great cultural importance, or finding a meaning you like and linking a name to it. The name Helen, for example, means 'light', but there are a great many variations of it, including Aileen, Eleanor, Helena and Lena. Therefore, if you like the idea of naming your daughter 'light' but aren't keen on Helen, researching other variations might just lead you to the perfect one.

- **Find a name with meaning.** When my parents discovered they were expecting a baby, they sought out possibilities that *meant* something. Both interested in history, they eventually settled on naming their three daughters after queens of England (Alexandra, Eleanor and Victoria) hoping to fill their children's souls with a sense of pride and importance. It worked, because throughout our lives we have all felt a duty to do our names justice in the modern world. Having a name which has a back story helps your child understand their significance in the world, so whether you name them after a religious saint or prophet, an important political figure or a hero in a Greek tragedy, ensure they know where their name came from. They may just be inspired to be as great as their namesake.

- **Have fun.** Picking out names should be a fun process. Laughing at the ones you'd never dream of choosing can really help you narrow it down to the ones you would. You can also experiment with different spellings, pronunciations or variations of names you like, or go to places where you might feel inspired. Some of the best names come from the worlds of nature and literature, so why not go down to your local garden centre or library and have fun with the classic, cute and downright silly words you find there?

- **Expand your mind**. Don't rule out the weird ones just yet! As a teenager I went to school with a girl named Siam. Her parents had conceived her on a honeymoon trip to Thailand and given her the country's old name as a result. She loved growing up and having an unusual name, as I'm sure Brooklyn Beckham (Posh and Becks's son) and Bronx Wentz (Ashley Simpson and Pete Wentz's son) do too. Also, don't be afraid to play around with spellings and pronunciations, even if the results are a little less than conformist. The name Madison, for example, could be spelt Maddison, Madyson, Maddiesun or even Maddeesunn if you so choose, although you might want to be careful you don't saddle your child with an impossible name to spell, pronounce *and* fit onto a passport application form.

You will want to pick a name that you can shout with confidence across the school playground, or hear with pride when they graduate from university. Pick a name which makes you smile because if you love it, hopefully your child will too.

- **Try it out.** While you're pregnant, talk to your baby and address it using a variety of your favourite names to see if it responds. There are numerous stories of names being chosen because the baby kicked when it was called Charlie or Aisha, but was suspiciously silent when it was called Dexter or Mildred, so see if it has a preference! You can also try writing names down and sticking them to your fridge, or saying one out loud enough times to see if you ever get sick of it. That name you picked out when you were eight and always said you'd name your first child, for example, might not sound so appropriate now you're an adult and have to name a human being for real.

- **What if you can't agree?** This is probably the trickiest problem in the baby-naming process to solve. It's wise to research a number of names you and your partner are both interested in and make a point of discussing your reasons for liking or disliking them long before the baby is due to be born. The labour and delivery room is probably not the best time to argue as you'll both be tired, emotional and at least one of you will be in pain. Avoid sticking to your guns on a name one of you really isn't happy with because it might lead to resentment down the line, with your baby caught in the middle. You could try compromising and picking two middle names so you both have a name in there you love, or you could each have five names you're allowed to 'veto' but no more. You could also try making contractions out of names you both like, such as Anna and Lisa (Annalisa) or James and Hayden (Jayden). Whichever way you go about it, it is important that you both eventually agree on the name you are giving your baby, even if it means losing out on that one you've had your heart set on for a while.

Spanish names for boys and girls

- Alejandro
- Carlos
- Diego
- Ivan
- Javier
- Jorge
- Marcos
- Mario
- Pablo
- Raul

- Ana
- Carla
- Carmen
- Daniela
- Elena
- Marina
- Maria
- Natalia
- Sara
- Sophia

French names for boys and girls

- Alain
- Gerard
- Luc
- Jean
- Louis
- Alphonse
- Jacques
- Marc
- Matthieu
- Guy

- Adele
- Belle
- Fleur
- Paulette
- Sabine
- Amelie
- Colette
- Giselle
- Yvette
- Monique

Things to consider when naming

Thinking to the future

> From our ancestors come our names, but from our virtues our honours.

Proverb

One important aspect of naming your child is thinking ahead to their future. Will the name you've chosen stand the test of time? Will names popular in 2011 remain popular in 2035? Will they be able to confidently enter a room and give a crucial business presentation with an awkward or unpronounceable name? Will they be able to hand their business card over to a potential client without that client looking bemused every time? Even on a smaller scale, can they survive the potential minefields of primary and secondary school with a name that could be easily shortened to something embarrassing?

While it seems a very long way off now, it is important to think about the impact your chosen name will have on your child's life, and how they will cope with that name as an adult. Introducing themselves as Professor Xavier to a group of university deans might raise a few smirks among knowing *X-Men* fans, as would any unusual or trendy 2011 name which has lost its shine by 2035. Would you want to try catching criminals as Police Officer Apple Blossom or have other politicians take you seriously with a name like MP Lil' Kim Scarlett? You don't want to give your child a name which they just cannot live with for the rest of their lives, so make your choice based on what's appropriate for a child as well as an adult. To make this easier you might want to choose a longer name which can be shortened or extended as your child desires.

Banned names

The following names were all banned by registration officials in New Zealand:

- Cinderella Beauty Blosson
- Fat Boy
- Fish and Chips (twins)
- Keenan Got Lucy
- O.crnia
- Sex Fruit
- Stallion
- Talula Does The Hula From Hawaii
- Twisty Poi
- Yeah Detroit

This was because New Zealand law prevents parents from giving their children names which would cause offence or are more than 100 characters long.

Allowed names

These names, however, were all permitted by the same officials:

- All Blacks
- Benson and Hedges (twins)
- Ford Mustang
- Kaos
- Masport and Mower (twins)
- Midnight Chardonnay
- Number 16 Bus Shelter
- Spiral Cicada
- Superman (changed from 4real)
- Violence

Nicknames

> Of all eloquence a nickname is the most concise; of all arguments the most unanswerable.

William Hazlitt

Nicknames are an unavoidable part of the history of names. Even seemingly simple names which do not lend themselves to being shortened can be subject to it: Prince Harry's real name, for example, is actually Henry, but he has been referred to as Harry since birth.

Nicknames can range from the common – Mike from Michael, Sam from Samantha – to the trendy, funny or downright insulting. My husband's brother was known as 'JoBi Wan Kenobi' from a very young age thanks to being given the name Joseph and I've lost count of the number of Richards who refuse to be called 'Dick' or the Francescas who prefer 'Fran' over 'Fanny'.

The first time your child encounters a nickname will probably be before they're even born, or at least within the first few months. Many older siblings find new names hard to remember or pronounce and your baby could end up with a nickname before you know it. As an infant myself I was referred to as 'Baby Turner' by my older sister for the first few weeks, followed by 'Nell' once she realised I had a real name but couldn't say it properly. 'Nell' stuck from that moment on, and my family still find it difficult to call me by my full name when I visit them, despite my many protestations. If your baby has an older sibling, try talking to them about their new brother or sister using the name you've chosen so you can discover how their imagination might choose to interpret it. If they're an older child you might even want to include them in the naming process from the start, if for no other reason than they mention a friend at school who gets teased for having an unfortunate nickname derived from the name you've chosen.

With all this said however, it is perfectly possible to choose a name which you know has an unfortunate nickname associated with it but for it to not bother you. If you don't encourage the use of nicknames when your child is young, chances are one won't stick when they're older either. I, for example, don't tell anyone I meet as an adult that I was known as Nell for the better half of my childhood, so no-one calls me that now. Another way to avoid embarrassing nicknames is to select one for your child that you actually like so that others don't even get a mention. Call your daughter Elizabeth by Liz, Lizzie or Libby if you don't like Betty or Beth, and no-one will even consider the alternatives.

You can pre-empt problem nicknames to some extent by saying the name you've chosen out loud and trying to find rhymes for it. This is a clever way to avoid playground chants and nursery rhyme-type insults, such as Andy Pandy or Looby Lou. It is a sad truth though that children will rhyme anything with anything else if they can, so while you might wish to take playground chants into account during your naming process, don't be too concerned about them. Most children are subjected to it at some point and emerge unscathed.

A Chinese couple were prevented from naming their child '@' in 2007, despite their reasoning that it was simply a modern choice of name in this technological age.

Initials

What surname will your baby have? Does its first letter lend itself easily to amusing acronyms already, and would choosing certain forenames only exacerbate the problem? If your child will inherit a double-barrelled surname this becomes a bigger consideration still, as there are more amusing four letter words than there are three. My brother-in-law was going to be called Andrew Steven Schmitt before he was born, until his parents realised at the last minute what his initials would spell...

It's worth taking the time to think about acronyms of initials in the real world too, such as how credit cards display names or seeing your child's name written out on a form. Nobody should have to go through life known as Earl E. Bird, I. P. Freely or S. Lugg because their parents didn't think that far ahead. For a wonderful selection of these types of names, tune in to *The Simpsons* and observe Bart's prank phone calls to Moe's Tavern.

Amusing initials

- Earl E. Bird
- Kay F. Cee
- I. P. Freely
- Al E. Gador
- Angie O. Graham
- S. Lugg
- Warren T.
- I.C. Blood
- H. I. Vee
- Gene E. Yuss

Amusing acronyms of real people

- Samuel Alan Spencer – SAS
- Neil Christopher Parker – NCP (the car park)
- James John Brookes – JJB (the sportswear shop)
- Jake Clive Baxter – JCB
- Patricia Mary Simpson – PMS
- David Vernon Durante – DVD
- Victoria Helen Smith – VHS
- Jennifer Paige Garrett – JPG
- George Barry Holmes – GBH

Your surname

Connected to your child's potential new initials is their
new surname. Whether they are receiving their name from
their mother, father or a hyphenated combination of both,
matching an appropriate first name to their surname is an
important undertaking. Try to avoid forenames which might
lead to unfortunate phrases when combined with certain
surnames to prevent a lifetime of embarrassment for your
baby. The best way to work out if this might happen is to
write down all the names you like alongside your child's
last name and have someone else read them out loud. This
second pair of eyes and ears might just spot something you
didn't.

Unfortunate forename/surname combinations

- Anna Sasin
- Barb Dwyer
- Barry Cade
- Ben Dover
- Duane Pipe
- Grace Land
- Harry Rump
- Hazel Nutt
- Isabella Horn
- Jenny Taylor
- Justin Time
- Mary Christmas
- Oliver Sutton
- Paige Turner
- Russell Sprout
- Stan Still
- Teresa Green

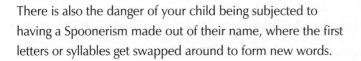

There is also the danger of your child being subjected to
having a Spoonerism made out of their name, where the first
letters or syllables get swapped around to form new words.

An unfortunate and recent example of this would be Angelina Jolie and Brad Pitt's daughter Shiloh, whom they named Shiloh Jolie-Pitt to avoid the inevitable Shiloh Pitt Spoonerism. Try to avoid making the same mistake!

French law prohibits all names other than those on an approved list.

Quirky names and stereotypes

There are lots of disadvantages to having a quirky name, but there are plenty of advantages too. For one thing, your child's name will never be forgotten by other people, and if they do something influential with their life their name could become inspirational for other parents to name their children. On the other hand, a quirky name often requires a quirky personality. If you don't think your genes could stand up to a name like Satchel or Kerensa, perhaps it's time to think of one a little more run-of-the-mill.

A quirky name often says more about the parents than the child, whose own personalities may affect the personality of their child in a significant way. A conventional family who name their baby John will probably find he becomes a conventional child, whereas a quirky family who name their baby Zanzibar will also find he develops a quirky personality. The name itself is not the leading factor; it's the quirky or conventional behaviour encouraged by the parents who chose the name that is.

It is not true that babies are as influenced by their names as people believe. There is no scientific evidence to say that names dictate who we become, which means that you cannot give your child a perfect or imperfect name, whichever one you finally pick.

What is usually the case is that people make assumptions about a name and that person's personality lives up to or fails those expectations. A boy named William might be expected to be intelligent, whereas one named Attila will be viewed automatically as a bully. A girl named Norma might be told her name is too old for her and one named Honey might be told it's too young. None of these assumptions, however, will change the personality of your child one iota, so if you want to choose a quirky name for them feel free to do so.

Assumptions about names

Research has shown that most people do make assumptions based on a person's name. A 2009 survey found that 49% of teachers make assumptions about their pupils based on their name. One in three admitted that certain names spell a troublemaker to them, including Callum, Brandon, Chelsea and Aleisha, while the names Christopher, Edward, Rebecca and Charlotte were assumed to belong to brighter children. Of course these assumptions vanish as soon as teachers meet their pupils but you know what they say about first impressions!

Names from fictional characters

The one type of quirky name you may wish to pause and consider is that of fictional characters, especially cartoon characters. Your baby is highly likely to be exposed to cartoons before they start school, so they will have their name associated with whatever their peers have read or seen. A boy named Barney or Fred, for example, might be teased for having the same name as a giant purple dinosaur or a Stone Age cartoon character. A girl named Ariel or Belle might be expected to behave like a little princess, while one named Dorothy might be constantly asked if she wants to go home…

While avoiding any kind of possible connection to a fictional character is nigh on impossible, you can help make things easier for your child by educating them about their namesake and encouraging them to read more about them. Stay up-to-date with new cartoons and children's characters in 2011 to prepare both yourself and your child for toddlerdom and childhood. That way they can be proud of their name and have ammunition if things get rough in the playground.

If you need inspiration why not try following the latest trend from the States and consider a character from your favourite book or film? The names Edward, Isabella and Jacob have all leapt in popularity since the release of *Twilight* by Stephanie Meyer. Even surnames of these characters have increased in popularity: the name Cullen jumped 300 places in a single year.

Using family names

Some families have a strong tradition of using names for babies that come from the family tree. There are instances where naming your son Augustine VIII is simply not an option; it's a rule. Another way families do this is to give children the name of their parent of the same sex and add 'Junior' (Jr.) to the end. This could potentially create a problem if that child then decides to carry on the tradition and name their child after themselves – after all, who wants to be known as Frederick Jr. Jr.?

There are obviously pros and cons with using family names:

- Pro: Your child will feel part of a strong tradition, which will create a sense of security for them and help make them feel a complete member of the family.

- Pro: If you're having a problem selecting a name you and your partner both agree on, this is a very simple solution and will make your new child's family very happy.

- Con: You might not actually like the name that's being passed down. Naming your child the 12th Thumbelina in a row might not actually hold the same attraction for you as for the generation before you.

- Con: Another drawback could be if the cultural associations with that name have changed in your lifetime and it is no longer appropriate.

One way to navigate around choosing a family name is to compromise. You could use the name as a middle name, or refer to your baby by a nickname instead. You could also suggest using a name from the other partner's family: if the name comes from your side, try finding one you like from the other side. If their argument is for tradition then this is an astonishingly effective counter-argument.

Whatever you decide about using family names, just remember that this is *your* baby. Just as your parents got to decide what they named you, you get to decide this. If family and friends are disappointed, don't be alarmed. Once the baby is here they will only see how much she has her grandmother's nose, or his grandfather's ears, and the name will become far less important.

Some old-fashioned names for boys and girls

- Henry
- Charlie
- William
- Joseph
- Arthur
- Fred
- Harry
- Edward
- Julian
- Miles

- Ava
- Grace
- Mary
- Olivia
- Rosemary
- Elizabeth
- Margaret
- Louisa
- Martha
- Dorothy

Spellings and pronunciation

Once you've finally agreed upon a name, it's time to consider how you wish it to be spelt and pronounced. Some parents take great joy in experimenting with unusual variations of traditional names, while others prefer for names to be instantly recognisable. The only advice here is to use caution in your experiments. There are many anecdotal tales of parents seeing or hearing pretty names in the hospital during delivery and choosing them for their children, only to find out later they were medical terms and therefore completely inappropriate as names. Even spelling or pronouncing them differently won't be of much use once they're old enough to know the meaning behind them.

Actual medical terms used as names

- Arsehole (pronounced ar-SHOL-ee)
- Chlamydia
- Eczema
- Female (pronounced fuh-MAH-lee)
- Latrine (pronounced lah-TREE-nee)
- Meconium
- Syphilis
- Testicles (pronounced TESS-tee-clees)
- Urine (pronounced yer-REE-nee)
- Vagina (pronounced vaj-EE-nah)

Obviously the examples above are a little extreme, but the choices you make regarding spelling and pronunciation are really important. Try to avoid making a common name too long or too unusual in its spelling as this will be the first thing your child learns how to write. They will also be subjected to constant corrections during their lifetime, as other people misspell or mispronounce their name in ever more frustrating patterns. Make sure the name isn't too long that it won't fit on forms or name badges as they'll simply stop using it and take on a nickname instead. Substituting the odd 'i' for a 'y' isn't too bad, but turning the name Jonathan into Jonnaythanne doesn't do anyone any favours.

Britain has seen an increase in 'text' language spellings

- An
- Camron
- Conna
- Ema
- Esta
- Flicity
- Helin
- Jaicub
- Jayk
- Lora
- Patryk
- Samiul
- Summa

Middle names

The use of middle names is generally acknowledged to be standard practice in the UK these days. In fact, it has become fairly uncommon to name a child *without* a middle name, although there are cultures where this is still the case. A middle name can have just as much of an impact as a forename so your choice for your own baby should be made as carefully as their first name.

You may have already decided what middle name to give your child due to tradition or culture, in which case the following advice may be moot. In Spanish cultures, for example, middle names are often the mother's surname or other name to promote that matriarchal lineage. Similarly, parents who have not taken each other's surnames or are not married may choose to give their child one surname as a middle name and one as a last name so both parents are represented. Other traditions may use an old family name, passed down to each first-born son or daughter to encourage a sense of family pride and history. A decision about what middle name to pass on may have therefore already been made for you, even before your own birth.

If you are choosing a middle name there are some common trends in 2011 to help you narrow it down.

- **Opposite-length names**. It has become very popular to give a child either a long forename and short middle name, or a short forename and long middle name. If this idea attracts you, consider using syllables to give you an idea of length and combinations.
  - o Generally, if the forename has only one or two syllables (Owen, Steven, Yasmin, Zoe) then the middle name can have two, three or even four syllables (Owen Henri, Steven Michael, Yasmin Samantha, Zoe Jessica).
  - o If the opposite is true and the forename is three or four syllables long (Anthony, Jennifer, Nicholas, Rosemary), the middle name may be better kept to

only one or two syllables (Anthony Kevin, Jennifer Ruth, Nicholas John, Rosemary Dawn). Of course, this rule may need to be tailored to your child's last name as a very long or hyphenated surname may suit a different combination entirely.

The shortest baby names are only two letters long (Al, Ed, Jo and Ty), but the longest could be any length imaginable. Popular 11 letter-long names include Bartholomew, Christopher, Constantine and Maximillian.

- **Name from the family tree**. Honouring your ancestors is another popular trend for 2011. Parents are frequently looking back to their own lineage for interesting, unusual or influential names.
  - o If you know you or your partner is related to Charles Darwin, you might choose Charles or even Darwin as a middle name for your son, or if your great-great-grandmother had a particularly unusual name and worked in the Suffragette movement, you could choose her name for your daughter's middle name.
  - o If a relative passed away recently you could choose their name as a way of honouring their memory, or you could even choose it while they're still alive to make them proud.
  - o It is becoming more and more common to give a parents' first name as a middle name to newborns.

- **Unusual names**. Along with a wider variety of first names in recent years (Ruby, Amelia and Mia have all climbed the Top 20 charts over the last five years, replacing the standard Emily, Chloe and Megan), parents are choosing more unusual middle names too. This would make sense, as a child named Bronte or Keilyn probably needs a fairly uncommon middle name to balance it out. Alternatively, as middle names are far less frequently used, this is an opportunity for parents to have an unusual name included that they wouldn't perhaps use otherwise. If their child grows up not to like it they have the option of only using their initial, or simply dropping it from daily use altogether.

- **Common names**. As a last resort, if you find you are struggling to pick a middle name you could always pick a traditionally used one. For girls, Anne, Marie, May and Rose have all been strikingly popular in 2010 and 2011 and the same is true for Andrew, David, James and Thomas for boys.

Popular middle names for boys in 2011

- Adam
- Alexander
- Andrew
- David
- James

- Joseph
- Lee
- Michael
- Steven
- Thomas

Popular middle names for girls in 2011

- Anne
- Elise
- Elizabeth
- Grace
- Louise
- Marie
- May
- Nicole
- Rose
- Ruth

As with first names, middle names can have hilarious consequences if not thought about carefully. It's worth writing down your favourite combinations and saying them out loud to make sure you're not making one of these mistakes:

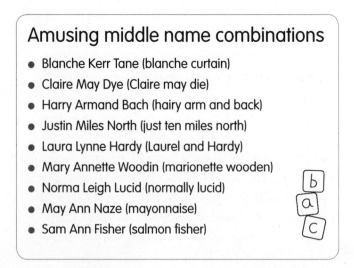

Amusing middle name combinations

- Blanche Kerr Tane (blanche curtain)
- Claire May Dye (Claire may die)
- Harry Armand Bach (hairy arm and back)
- Justin Miles North (just ten miles north)
- Laura Lynne Hardy (Laurel and Hardy)
- Mary Annette Woodin (marionette wooden)
- Norma Leigh Lucid (normally lucid)
- May Ann Naze (mayonnaise)
- Sam Ann Fisher (salmon fisher)

Of course, you don't have to narrow down middle name choices to just one. It is becoming more and more common to have several middle names, particularly if parents like more than one or want to include a family name as well. Be careful not to have too many though, as this makes life very difficult when filling out official forms or enrolling your child in school. Most institutions only recognise one middle name, and some only recognise a middle initial.

The Glastonbury teenager named **Captain Fantastic Faster Than Superman Spiderman Batman Wolverine Hulk And The Flash Combined**, changed his name from George Garratt in 2008. He claims to have the longest name in the world. If he does then he replaces Texan woman **Rhoshandiatellyneshiaunneveshenk Koyaanisquatsiuth Williams**, whose 57-letter length name pales in comparison to Captain's 81.

One last thing to bear in mind when choosing a middle name is that many people actually choose to go by this name instead of their forename. Celebrities often do this so they can be identified separately to other people of the same name (Michael Keaton's real name is Michael Douglas, for example), but it is just as common for non-celebrities too. In fact, you probably know someone in your family or workplace that has always been known as Ed or Sam when their name is actually James Edward Jones or Felicity Samantha Taylor. You might even choose to do this with your own child, particularly if you're using a family name and adding Jr. to the title. It might be easier to call James Jones Jr. Ed, if only to make it clear who you're telling off at the dinner table!

Celebrities who go by middle names

- Antonio Banderas (Jose Antonio Dominguez Banderas)
- Bob Marley (Nesta Robert Marley)
- Dakota Fanning (Hannah Dakota Fanning)
- Will Ferrell (John William Ferrell)
- Kelsey Grammer (Allen Kelsey Grammer)
- Ashton Kutcher (Christopher Ashton Kutcher)
- Hugh Laurie (James Hugh Calum Laurie)
- Evangeline Lilly (Nicole Evangeline Lilly)
- Brad Pitt (William Bradley Pitt)
- Brooke Shields (Christa Brooke Camille Shields)
- Reese Witherspoon (Laura Jean Reese Witherspoon)

The science of baby naming

> Always end the name of your child with a vowel, so that when you yell the name will carry.

Bill Cosby

Whether you agree with it or not, there is a certain science to naming babies. Even at the very basic level of choosing a name you like the sound of, the science is there.

Some experts have noted that parents who choose inspirational names for their offspring (Destiny, Serenity,

Unique) or names of products they aspire to own (Armani, Jaguar, Mercedes) are projecting a future onto their child for them to aspire to. After all, the idea of a Mercedes working at a local fast-food restaurant isn't nearly as attractive as one who works as a lawyer or artist.

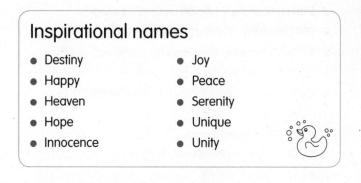

Inspirational names

- Destiny
- Happy
- Heaven
- Hope
- Innocence
- Joy
- Peace
- Serenity
- Unique
- Unity

Future aspirations names

- Armani
- Aston
- Bugatti
- Chanel
- Dolce
- Ferrari
- Jaguar
- Mercedes
- Porsche
- Prada

Names of US Presidents

- Abraham (Lincoln)
- Andrew (Jackson, Johnson)
- Barack (Obama)
- Franklin (Pierce, Roosevelt)
- George (Washington, H. Bush, W. Bush)
- James (Madison, Monroe, Knox Polk, Buchanan, Garfield, Carter)
- John (Adams, Quincy Adams, Tyler, Kennedy)
- Richard (Nixon)
- Ronald (Reagan)
- William (Henry Harrison, McKinley, Howard Taft, Clinton)

Names of UK Prime Ministers

- Anthony (Eden, Blair)
- Arthur (Wellesley, Balfour)
- David (Cameron, Lloyd George)
- Charles (Wentworth, Grey)
- George (Grenville, Canning, Gordon)
- Gordon (Brown)
- Harold (Macmillan, Wilson)
- Henry (Pelham, Fitzroy, Addington, Temple, Campbell-Bannerman, Asquith)
- John (Stuart, Russell, Major)
- Robert (Walpole, Jenkinson, Peel, Gascoyne-Cecil)
- Spencer (Compton, Perceval)
- William (Cavendish, Pitt (Elder and Younger), Wyndham, Lamb, Gladstone)

While parents are often cautioned or even discouraged from picking wild and crazy names for their babies (think about Petal Blossom Rainbow, Jamie Oliver's third daughter) there isn't actually any scientific evidence to suggest that children are hindered in any way by them. There seems to be more evidence to suggest that the stories behind names are more important.

Children who are told they have inherited an ancestor's name or that of an influential character from history seem to be more driven and focused than children who are told disappointingly, 'We just liked the sound of it'. As a parent, therefore, it seems it's okay to pick an unusual name if you have the story or anecdotal evidence to back it up.

Another thing to consider about the science of baby naming is how your child's name will be perceived by the outside world. Typically, judgements are passed on names before a person is met, such as at job interviews or in school. This does have the potential to hold back your child, although there is conflicting evidence to say that once someone is met in person, assumptions and stereotypes are wiped away.

Personality and character have a far greater influence than name alone and after a while, a name becomes just a name.

It is wise to be cautious though, particularly if the name you're considering is extremely controversial. In the United States in December 2008 there was a case of a supermarket bakery refusing to ice the words 'Happy Birthday, Adolf Hitler' onto a three year old's birthday cake, despite never having met the child it was intended for. The parents were able to eventually fulfil the order at another shop, but as a result of the publicity surrounding the event Social Services were called in to assess the child's home and Adolf, along with his siblings JoyceLynn Aryan Nation and Honszlynn Hinler Jeannie, were taken into care and we have already seen the beginning of this with Mohammed entering the Top 10 for the first time.

Controversial names adopted by real people

- Adolf Hitler
- Beelzebub
- Desdemona
- Hannibal Lecter
- Himmler

- Jezebel
- Lucifer
- Mussolini
- Stalin
- Voldemort

If your child will be given a name from an ethnic or cultural heritage, there is often a fear that this will potentially hold them back. Many children from a Chinese heritage, for example, choose to adopt a Western name while at school rather than have countless teachers and classmates mispronounce or make judgements about their name.

Another example would be strong Islamic names (think Ahmed, Mohammed or Neha), which given the current political climate, some children and teenagers fear could prevent them from being treated fairly at school or in their first job. This is not to say that these names should not be used, as it is the fault of prejudiced people passing judgements on your child's name rather than the fault of the name itself. In fact, the greater the diversity of names and cultures represented by them, the greater the chance of society's acceptance overall, and we have already seen the beginning of this with Mohammed entering the top 10 for the first time.

4

Registering a baby name

There are slightly different guidelines for registering births and names depending on where you live in the UK:

- **In England, Wales and Northern Ireland** a birth must be recorded within 42 days of delivery and if not done at the hospital it requires a visit to a register office.

- The birth certificate will be written in English if a child is born in England or Northern Ireland, and can be in both English and Welsh if they are born in Wales.

- If your baby is recorded at the hospital or in the same district as the birth itself then birth certificates are usually issued straight away, but if you end up going to a different office the certificate may be sent to you after a few days. This is important when applying for Child Benefits or registering your baby with a doctor as you will need a copy of the short birth certificate to apply.

- If the parents of a newborn are married, either parent can register a birth. However, if the parents are not married there are several ways to ensure both names are put on the birth certificate, including both parents being physically present at the registration or one parent submitting a declaration form in lieu of their presence. If neither parent can be present then someone who was present at the birth or someone who is now responsible for the child can also carry out the duty.

- After the registration parents or those with parental responsibility also have the option of requesting a naming ceremony. These non-religious ceremonies are conducted by local authorities and can be a nice replacement for a baptism or Christening as adults outside of the family can be nominated to act in secular roles similar to God Parents. A birth certificate is also needed for this event to take place.

- **In Scotland** births need to be registered within 21 days and can take place in any district. As well as either married parents being allowed to register the birth, relatives of those parents may also do the duty. The exception here is if the parents are not married. In this case the father may only register the birth if the mother is also present, a declaration form is submitted or a court agrees that he has parental responsibility just like any other adult. Parents of newborns in Scotland should take a card given to them at the hospital and a copy of their marriage certificate to the birth registration.

Useful websites:

Registering a birth in England and Wales: www.direct.gov.uk
Registering a birth in Northern Ireland: www.groni.gov.uk
Registering a birth in Scotland: www.gro-scotland.gov.uk

German law prohibits invented and androgynous names but the UK has some of the most liberal rules on naming a baby in the world, with only names which are deemed to be offensive making it onto the banned list.

If you decide at a later stage you want to change details on the birth certificate there are procedures in place to help, although it is often a time-consuming process.

- It is worth remembering that if the father's details were not recorded on the original certificate or if the natural parents have married since the registration, a new birth certificate will have to be generated. Both changes require filling out an application form, available on the websites listed above.

- If you are unhappy with the forename you've chosen or it has been spelt incorrectly you can change the birth record providing you have other documentation to prove this is the case. A passport or baptismal certificate is sufficient as they will show the correct spelling or commonly used forename and should be presented to the register office where the initial application was made.

- If you wish to change the surname of your baby it is only possible in two cases: either the spelling is incorrect or the details of the parents are being changed (such as the inclusion of the father or the parents now being married). Again, evidence and form submissions are needed to make any changes and a fee is usually incurred if a new certificate is required.

Keep in mind how difficult it may be for you to change your child's birth certificate at a later stage if you are in any way unsure about the choice you're about to make. However, also remember that if something unexpected happens and you need to make the change, it is possible. There are stories of drunken fathers registering the birth of their child alone with a name not agreed upon by the mother, much to her horror. As Robert Eisenschmidt says, 'I have a friend, Bill Land, who named his daughter Alison Wanda Land. His wife changed the name on the birth certificate when she found out.' So it is possible, though obviously not preferred.

5

Naming twins, triplets and more

If you have discovered you are expecting multiples, congratulations! Naming multiples needn't be any different to naming a single child... unless you want it to be. You could stick to the same process everyone else does, by picking an individual name for each individual child, or you could go with a theme. Try anagrams or names in reverse, or give each child the same initials. You could even do this if you're not expecting multiples, like the Duggar family of Arkansas, USA, who have given each of their 19 children the initial 'J'.

Twin anagram combinations

- Blake and Kaleb
- Dean and Aden
- Edna and Dena
- Ira and Ria
- Johan and Jonah
- Lisa and Ilsa
- Mary and Myra
- Moira and Mario
- Noel and Leon
- Reva and Vera

A palindrome name is a name which is spelt the same backwards and forwards, as with Bob, Elle, Eve and Hannah.

Twin names with the same meaning

- Bernard and Brian (strong)
- Daphne and Laura (laurel)
- Deborah and Melissa (bee)
- Dorcas and Tabitha (gazelle)
- Elijah and Joel (God)
- Eve and Zoe (life)
- Irene and Salome (peace)
- Lucius and Uri (light)
- Lucy and Helen (light)
- Sarah and Almira (princess)

Popular twin names in 2010

- Brandon and Brian
- Daniel and David
- Ella and Emma
- Faith and Hope
- Gabriella and Isabella
- Isaac and Isaiah
- Jacob and Joshua
- Madison and Morgan
- Matthew and Michael
- Taylor and Tyler

Of course, when all is said and done you can just stick to giving each child a name unique to them. For triplets, quads and more this is probably an easier choice than twisting your head around three names with the same meaning, or trying to create four anagrams you like for all of your babies. Some parents do like to use a theme though, such as matching initials or names that go down the alphabet (think Alastair, Benjamin, Christopher and David).

The likelihood of women conceiving multiples in the 21st century is on the rise, which experts have attributed to couples delaying having children until later in life (women over 30 are more likely to have multiples) and more couples having access to affordable fertility treatments (fertility drugs have a higher rate of multiple-birth pregnancies than normal). It's also becoming very common for celebrities to have multiple births these days, for exactly the same reasons as the rest of us. However, not all of them have stuck to a theme with names.

Nadya Suleman, also known as Octomom, is the most famous recent example of a mother with a multiple pregnancy. Nadya chose eight different names for her octuplets born in January 2009; Isaiah, Jeremiah, Jonah, Josiah, Maliah, McCai, Nariah and Noah; the babies all share the middle name Angel though so that might make things a little easier!

Celebrity twin names of the past few years

- Darby and Sullivan (Patrick Dempsey and Jillian Fink)
- Anton and Olivia (Al Pacino and Beverly D'Angelo)
- Eden and Savannah (Marcia Cross and Tom Mahoney)
- D'Lila Star and Jessie James (P Diddy and Kim Porter)
- Hazel and Phinnaeus (Julia Roberts and Danny Moder)
- Thomas Boone and Zoe Grace (Dennis and Kimberley Quaid)
- Marion Loretta and Tabitha Hodge (Sarah Jessica Parker and Matthew Broderick)
- Max and Bob (Charlie Sheen and Brooke Mueller)
- Max and Emme (Jennifer Lopez and Marc Anthony)
- Vivienne Marcheline and Knox Leon (Angelina Jolie and Brad Pitt)

Names for triplets

- Abel, Bela and Elba (anagrams)
- Aidan, Diana and Nadia (anagrams)
- April, May and June (months)
- Amber, Jade and Ruby (jewels)
- Amy, May and Mya (anagrams)
- Ava, Eva and Iva (similar)
- Daisy, Lily and Rose (flowers)
- Jay, Raven and Robin (birds)
- Leah, Lianne and Liam (similar)
- Olive, Violet and Sage (colours)

part two

Boys' Names

A

Boys' names

Aaron

Hebrew, meaning 'mountain of strength'.

Abasi

Egyptian, meaning 'male'.

Abdiel

Biblical, meaning 'servant of God'.

Abdul

Arabic, meaning 'servant'. Often followed with a suffix indicating who Abdul is the servant of (eg Abdul-Basit, 'servant of the creator').

Abdullah

Arabic, meaning 'servant of God'.

Abe

Hebrew, from Abraham, meaning 'father'.

Abel

Hebrew, meaning 'breath' or 'breathing spirit'. Associated with the Biblical son of Adam and Eve who was killed by his brother Cain.

Abelard

German, meaning 'resolute'.

Aberforth

Gaelic, meaning 'mouth of the river Forth'. Name of Dumbledore's brother in the *Harry Potter* books.

A

Abheek
Indian, meaning 'fearless'.

Abhishek
Indian, meaning 'bath for a deity' or 'anointing'.

Abner
Biblical Hebrew, meaning 'father of light'.

Absalom
(alt. Absalon)
Hebrew, meaning 'father/ leader of peace'.

Acacio
Greek origin, meaning 'thorny tree'. Now widely used in Spain.

Ace
English, meaning 'number one' or 'the best'.

Achilles
Greek. Mythological hero of the Trojan war, whose heel was his only weak spot.

Achim
Hebrew, meaning 'God will establish' or Polish, meaning 'the Lord exalts'.

Ackerley
Old English, meaning 'oak meadow'. Often used as surname.

Adalberto
Germanic/Spanish, meaning 'nobly bright'.

Adam
Hebrew, meaning 'man' or 'earth'. First man to walk the earth, accompanied by Eve.

Adão
Variant of Adam, meaning 'earth'.

Addison
Old English, meaning 'son of Adam'. Also used as a female name in the USA.

Ade
African, meaning 'peak' or 'pinnacle'.

A

Adelard

Teutonic, meaning 'brave' or 'noble'.

Adelbert

Old German form of Albert.

Aden

Gaelic, meaning 'fire'.

Adetokunbo

Yoruba, meaning 'the crown came from over the sea'.

Adin

Hebrew, meaning 'slender' or 'voluptuous'. Also Swahili, meaning 'ornamental'.

Aditya

Sanskrit, meaning 'belonging to the sun'.

Adlai

Hebrew, meaning 'God is just', or sometimes 'ornamental'.

Adler

Old German, meaning 'eagle'.

Adley

English, meaning 'son of Adam'.

Admon

Hebrew origin, variant of Adam meaning 'earth'. Also the name of a red peony.

Adolph
(alt. Adolf)

Old German, meaning 'noble majestic wolf'. Popularity of the name plummeted after the Second World War, for obvious reasons.

Adonis

Phoenician, meaning 'Lord'.

Movie inspirations

Anakin (*Star Wars*)
Austin (*Austin Powers*)
Billy (*Kes*)
Don (*Singin' in the Rain*)
Jake (*Avatar*)
Korben (*The Fifth Element*)
Marty (*Back to the Future*)
Michael (*The Godfather*)
Renton (*Trainspotting*)
Ricky (*Casablanca*)
Wayne (*Wayne's World*)

A

Adrian

Latin origin, meaning 'from Hadria', a town in northern Italy.

Adriel

Biblical Hebrew, meaning 'of God's flock'.

Adyn
(alt. Adann, Ade, Aden)

Irish, meaning 'manly'.

Aeneas

Greek/Latin origin, meaning 'to praise'. Name of the hero who founded Rome in Virgil's *Aeneid*.

Aeson

Greek origin, father of Jason in Greek mythology.

Afonso

Portuguese, meaning 'eager noble warrior'.

Agamemnon

Greek. Figure in mythology, commanded the Greeks at the siege of Troy.

Agathon

Greek, meaning 'good' or 'superior'.

Agustin

Latin/Spanish, meaning 'venerated'.

Ahab

Hebrew, meaning 'father's brother'. Name of the obsessed captain in *Moby-Dick*.

Ahijah

Biblical Hebrew, meaning 'brother of God' or 'friend of God'.

Ahmed

Arabic/Turkish, meaning 'worthy of praise'.

Aidan

Gaelic, meaning 'little fire'.

Aidric

Old English, meaning 'oaken'.

Airyck

Old Norse, from Eric, meaning 'eternal ruler'.

A

Ajani

African, meaning 'he fights for what he is'. Also Sanskrit, meaning 'of noble birth'.

Ajax

Greek, meaning 'mourner of the Earth'. Another Greek hero from the siege of Troy.

Ajay

Indian, meaning 'unconquerable'.

Ajit

Indian, meaning 'invincible'.

Akeem

Arabic, meaning 'wise or insightful'.

Akio

Japanese, meaning 'bright man'.

Akira

Japanese, meaning 'intelligent'.

Akiva

Hebrew, meaning 'to protect' or 'to shelter'.

Akon

American, made popular by the famous rapper charting in 2008/2009.

Aksel

Hebrew/Danish, meaning 'father of peace'.

Aladdin

Arabic, meaning 'servant of Allah'. From the medieval Arabian story in *Arabian Nights*.

Alan

(alt. Allan, Allen, Allyn, Alun)

Gaelic, meaning 'rock'.

Alaric

Old German, meaning 'noble regal ruler'.

Alastair

(alt. Alasdair, Allister)

Greek/Gaelic, meaning 'defending men'.

Alban

Latin, meaning 'from Alba'. Also the name of Saint Alban, the first British Christian martyr.

A

Alberic

Germanic, meaning 'Elfin king'.

Albert

Old German, meaning 'noble, bright, famous'.

Albin

Latin, meaning 'white'.

Albus

Latin, variant of Albin meaning 'white'. Also the Christian name of Albus Dumbledore, headmaster of Hogwarts School in the *Harry Potter* books.

Alcaeus

Greek, meaning 'strength'.

Alden

Old English, meaning 'old friend'.

Aldis

English, meaning 'from the old house'.

Aldo

Italian origin, meaning 'old' or 'elder'.

Aldric

English, meaning 'old King'.

Alec

(alt. Alek)

English, meaning 'defending men'.

Aled

Welsh, meaning 'child' or 'offspring'.

Aleron

(alt. Aileron, Alerun, Ailerun)

Latin, meaning 'child with wings'.

Alessio

Italian, meaning 'defender'.

Alexander

(alt. Alex)

Greek origin, meaning 'defending men'.

Alexei

Russian origin, meaning 'defender'.

Alfonso

Germanic/Spanish, meaning 'noble and prompt, ready to struggle'.

A

Alford
Old English, meaning 'old river/ford'.

Alfred
(alt. Alf, Alfi)
English, meaning 'elf' or 'magical counsel'.

Algernon
French origin, meaning 'with a moustache'.

Ali
(alt. Allie)
Arabic, meaning 'noble, sublime'.

Alois
German, meaning 'famous warrior'.

Alok
Indian, meaning 'cry of triumph'.

Alon
Jewish, meaning 'oak tree'.

Alonso
(alt. Alonzo)
Germanic, meaning 'noble and ready'.

Aloysius
Italian saint's name, meaning 'fame and war'.

Alpha
First letter of the Greek alphabet.

Alphaeus
Hebrew origin, meaning 'changing'.

Alpin
Gaelic, meaning 'related to the Alps'.

Altair
Arabic, meaning 'flying' or 'bird'.

Alter
Yiddish, meaning 'old man'.

Alton
Old English, meaning 'old town'.

Alva
Latin, meaning 'white'.

A

Alvie

German, meaning 'army of elves'.

Alvin

English, meaning 'friend of elves'.

Alwyn

Welsh, meaning 'wise friend'. May also come from the River Alwen in Wales.

Amachi

African, meaning 'who knows what God has brought us through this child'.

Amadeus

Latin, meaning 'God's love'.

Amadi

African, meaning 'appeared destined to die at birth'.

Amado

Spanish, meaning 'God's love'.

Amador

Spanish, meaning 'one who loves'.

Amari

Hebrew, meaning 'given by God'.

Amarion

Arabic, meaning 'populous, flushing'.

Amasa

Hebrew, meaning 'burden'.

Ambrose

Greek, meaning 'undying, immortal'.

Americo

Germanic, meaning 'ever powerful in battle'.

Amias

Latin, meaning 'loved'.

Amil

African, meaning 'effective'.

Amir

Hebrew, meaning 'prince' or 'treetop'.

Amit

Hindu, meaning 'friend'.

A

Ammon

Egyptian, meaning 'the hidden one'.

Amory

German/English, meaning 'work' and 'power'.

Amos

Hebrew, meaning 'encumbered' or 'burdened'.

Anacletus

Latin, meaning 'called back' or 'invoked'.

Anakin

American, meaning 'warrior'. Made famous by Anakin Skywalker in the *Star Wars* films.

Ananias

Greek/Italian, meaning 'answered by the Lord'.

Anastasius

Latin, meaning 'resurrection'.

Anat

Jewish, meaning 'water spring'.

Anatole

Greek, meaning 'cynical but without malice'.

Anders

Greek, meaning 'lion man'.

Anderson

English, meaning 'male'.

Andrew
(alt. Andreas)

Greek, meaning 'man' or 'warrior'.

Androcles

Greek, meaning 'glory of a warrior'.

Angel

Greek, meaning 'messenger'.

Angus

Scottish, meaning 'one choice'.

Anil

Sanskrit, meaning 'air' or 'wind'.

Anselm

German, meaning 'helmet of God'.

A

Anson

English, meaning 'son of Agnes'.

Anthony

English, from the old Roman family name.

Antipas

Israeli, meaning 'for all or against all'.

Antwan

Old English, meaning 'flower'.

Apollo

Greek, meaning 'to destroy'. Greek god of the sun.

Apostolos

Greek, meaning 'apostle'.

Ara

Armenian. Ara was a legendary king.

Aragorn

Literary, used by Tolkien in *The Lord of the Rings* trilogy.

Aram

Biblical, meaning 'Royal Highness'.

Aramis

Latin, meaning 'swordsman'.

Arandu

Place in Pakistan, meaning 'little garden'.

Arcadio

Greek/Spanish, from a place in ancient Greece. The word 'Arcadia' (meaning paradise) comes from this.

Archibald
(alt. Archie)

Old German, meaning 'genuine/bold/brave'.

Ardell

Latin, meaning 'eager/burning with enthusiasm'.

Arden

Celtic, meaning 'high'.

Ares

Greek, meaning 'ruin'. Son of Zeus and Greek god of war.

A

Ari
Hebrew, meaning 'lion' or 'eagle'.

Arias
Germanic, meaning 'lion'.

Aric
English, meaning 'merciful ruler'.

Ariel
Hebrew, meaning 'lion of God'. One of the archangels, angel of healing and new beginnings.

Arild
Old Norse, meaning 'battle commander'.

Aris
Greek, meaning 'best figure'.

Ariston
Greek, meaning 'the best'.

Aristotle
Greek, meaning 'best'. Famous philosopher.

Arjun
Sanskrit, meaning 'white'.

Arkady
Greek, region of central Greece.

Arlan
Gaelic, meaning 'pledge' or 'oath'.

Arlie
Old English place name, meaning 'eagle wood'.

Arlis
Hebrew, meaning 'pledge'.

Arlo
Spanish, meaning 'barberry tree'.

Armand
Old German, meaning 'soldier'.

Armani
Same origin as Armand meaning 'soldier', nowadays closely associated with the Italian designer.

A

Arnaldo

Spanish, meaning 'eagle power'.

Arnav

Indian, meaning 'the sea'.

Arnold

Old German, meaning 'eagle ruler'.

Arrow

English, from the common word denoting weaponry.

Art

Irish, name of a warrior in Irish mythology, Art Oenfer (Art the Lonely).

Arthur

(alt. Artie, Artis)

Celtic, probably from 'artos', meaning 'bear'. Made famous by the tales of King Arthur and the Knights of the Round Table.

Arvel

From the Welsh 'Arwel', meaning 'wept over'.

Arvid

English, meaning 'eagle in the woods'.

Arvind

Indian, meaning 'red lotus'.

Arvo

Finnish, meaning 'value' or 'worth'.

Arwen

Welsh, meaning 'fair' or 'fine'.

Asa

Hebrew, meaning 'doctor' or 'healer'.

Asante

African, meaning 'thank you'.

Asher

Hebrew, meaning 'fortunate' or 'lucky'.

Ashley

Old English, meaning 'ash meadow'.

Ashok

Sanskrit, meaning 'not causing sorrow'.

A

Ashton

English, meaning 'settlement in the ash-tree grove'.

Aslan

Turkish, meaning 'lion'. Strongly associated with the lion from C S Lewis' *The Lion, the Witch, and the Wardrobe*.

Asriel

Biblical origin, meaning 'help of God'.

Astrophel

Latin, meaning 'star lover'.

Athanasios

Greek origin, meaning 'eternal life'.

Atílio

Portuguese, meaning 'father'.

Atlas

Greek, meaning 'to carry'. In Greek mythology Atlas was a Titan forced to carry the weight of the heavens.

Atlee

Hebrew, meaning 'God is just'.

Atticus

Latin, meaning 'from Athens'.

Literary names

Charlie (*Charlie and the Chocolate Factory*, Roald Dahl)
Christopher (*Now We Are Six*, A. A. Milne)
David (*David Copperfield*, Charles Dickens)
Gabriel (*Far from the Madding Crowd*, Thomas Hardy)
Dorian (*The Picture of Dorian Gray*, Oscar Wilde)
Ishmael (*Moby-Dick*, Herman Melville)
James (*James and the Giant Peach*, Roald Dahl)
Karin (*The Buddha of Suburbia*, Hanif Kureishi)
Phileas (*Around the World in Eighty Days*, Jules Verne)
Richard (*The Beach*, Alex Garland)
Winston (*Nineteen Eighty-Four*, George Orwell)

A

Auberon

Old German, meaning 'royal bear'.

Aubrey

Old German, meaning 'power'.

Auden

Old English, meaning 'old friend'.

Audie

Old English, meaning 'noble strength'.

Augustas
(alt. Augustus)

Latin, meaning 'venerated'.

Aurelien

French, meaning 'golden'.

Austin

Latin, meaning 'venerated'. Also city in the state of Texas in America.

Avi

Hebrew, meaning 'father of a multitude of nations'.

Avery
(alt. Avrie, Averey, Averie)

English, meaning 'wise ruler'.

Awnan

Irish, meaning 'little Adam'.

Axel

Hebrew, meaning 'father is peace'. Made famous by Guns 'n' Roses front man Axl Rose.

Ayers
(alt. Ayer, Aires, Aire)

English, meaning 'heir to a fortune'.

Azarel

Hebrew, meaning 'helped by God'.

Azaryah

Hebrew, meaning 'helped by God'.

Azriel

Hebrew, meaning 'God is my help'.

Azuko

African, meaning 'past glory'.

 **Boys' names**

Baden

German origin, meaning 'battle'.

Bailey

English, meaning 'bailiff'.

Baird

Scottish, meaning 'poet' or 'one who sings ballads'.

Bakari

Swahili, meaning 'hope' or 'promise'.

Baker

English, from the word baker.

Bakari

Swahili, meaning 'hope' or 'promise'.

Baldwin

Old French, meaning 'bold, brave friend'.

Balin

Old English. Balin was one of the knights of the Round Table.

Balthazar

Babylonian, meaning 'protect the King'.

Balvinder

Hindu, meaning 'merciful, compassionate'.

Bannon

Irish, descendant of O'Banain. Also a river in Wales.

B

Barack

African, meaning 'blessed'. Made popular by US President Barack Obama.

Barclay

Old English, meaning 'birch tree meadow'. Also Persian, meaning 'messenger'.

Barker

Old English, meaning 'shepherd'.

Barnaby
(alt. Barney)

Greek, meaning 'son of consolation'.

Barnard

English, meaning 'strong as a bear'.

Baron

Old English, meaning 'young warrior'.

Barrett

English, meaning 'strong as a bear'.

Barron

Old German, meaning 'old clearing'.

Barry

Irish Gaelic, meaning 'fair haired'. Also a town in South Wales, made popular by the BBC television series *Gavin and Stacey*.

Bart
(from Bartholomew)

Hebrew, meaning 'son of the farmer'. Made popular by the famous American TV character Bart Simpson.

Barton

Old English, meaning 'barley settlement'.

Baruch

Hebrew, meaning 'blessed'.

Barzillai

Hebrew, meaning 'my iron'.

Bashir

Arabic, meaning 'well-educated' and 'wise'.

B

Basil
Greek, meaning 'royal, kingly'.

Basim
Arabic, meaning 'smile'.

Bastien
Greek, meaning 'revered'.

Baxter
Old English, meaning 'baker'.

Bayard
French, meaning 'auburn haired'.

Bayre
American, meaning 'beautiful'.

Bayo
Nigerian, meaning 'to find joy'.

Baz
Irish Gaelic, meaning 'fair-haired'.

Beau
French, meaning 'handsome'.

Beck
Old Norse, meaning 'stream'.

Beckett
Old English, meaning 'beehive' or 'bee cottage'. Associated with the Irish writer Samuel Beckett.

Beckham
English, meaning 'homestead by the stream'. Made famous by David and Victoria Beckham.

Béla
Hungarian, meaning 'within'.

Belarius
Shakespearean, meaning 'a banished lord'.

Biblical names

Abel
Cain
Eli
Joseph
Luke
Mark
Moses
Paul
Peter
Solomon

B

Benedict

Latin, meaning 'blessed'.

Benicio

Spanish, meaning 'benevolent'.

Benjamin
(alt. Ben)

Hebrew, meaning 'son of the south'.

Bennett

French/Latin vernacular form of Benedict, meaning 'blessed'.

Benoit

French form of Benedict, meaning 'blessed'.

Benson

English, meaning 'son of Ben'. Also linked to the village of Benson in Oxfordshire.

Bentley

Old English, meaning 'bent grass meadow'.

Benton

Old English, meaning 'town in the bent grass'.

Beriah

Biblical, meaning 'in fellowship' or 'in envy'.

Bernard
(alt. Bernie)

Germanic, meaning 'strong, brave bear'.

Berry

Old English, meaning 'berry'.

Bert
(alt. Bertram/Bertrand)

Old English, meaning 'illustrious'.

Berton

Old English, meaning 'bright settlement'.

Bevan

Welsh, meaning 'son of Evan'.

Bilal

Arabic, meaning 'wetting, refreshing'.

Bill
(alt. Billy)

English, from William, meaning 'determined' or 'resolute'.

Birch

Old English, meaning 'bright' or 'shining'.

Birger

Norwegian, meaning 'rescue'.

Bishop

Old English, meaning 'bishop'.

Bjorn

Old Norse, meaning 'bear'.

Bladen

Hebrew, meaning 'hero'.

Blaine

Irish Gaelic, meaning 'yellow'.

Blair

English, meaning 'plain'.

Blaise

French, meaning 'lisp' or 'stutter'.

Blake

Old English, meaning 'dark, black'.

Blas

(alt. Blaze)

German, meaning 'firebrand'.

Bo

Scandinavian, short form of Robert, meaning 'bright fame'.

Boaz

Hebrew, meaning 'swiftness' or 'strength'.

Bob

(alt. Bobby)

From Robert, meaning 'bright fame'.

Boden

(alt. Bodie)

Scandinavian, meaning 'shelter'.

Bogumil

Slavic, meaning 'God favour'.

Bolivar

Spanish, meaning 'the bank of the river'.

Bond

Old English, meaning 'peasant farmer'.

B

Saints' names

Aidan
Bernard
Francis
Gabriel
Kieran
Nicholas
Patrick
Stephen
Thomas
Vincent

Boris

Slavic, meaning 'battle glory'.

Bosten

English, meaning 'town by the woods'.

Botolf

English, meaning 'wolf'.

Bowen

Welsh, meaning 'son of Owen'.

Boyd

Scottish Gaelic, meaning 'yellow'.

Brad
(alt. Bradley)

Old English, meaning 'broad' or 'wide'.

Brady

Irish, meaning 'large-chested'.

Bradyn

Gaelic, meaning 'descendant of Bradan'.

Bram

Gaelic, meaning 'raven'.

Brandon

Old English, meaning 'gorse'.

Brandt

Old English, meaning 'beacon'.

Brandy

English, meaning 'brandy'.

Brannon

Gaelic, meaning 'raven'.

Branson

English, meaning 'son of Brand'.

B

Brant
Old English, meaning 'hill'.

Braulio
Greek, meaning 'shining'.

Brendan
Gaelic, meaning 'prince'.

Brennan
Gaelic, meaning 'teardrop'.

Brenton
English, from Brent, meaning 'hill'.

Brett
English, meaning 'a brewer'.

Brewster
(alt. Brew, Brewer)
English, meaning 'a brewer'.

Brian
Gaelic, meaning 'high' or 'noble'.

Brice
Latin, meaning 'speckled'.

Brier
French, meaning 'heather'.

Brock
Old English, meaning 'badger'.

Broderick
English, meaning 'ruler'.

Brody
Gaelic, meaning both 'ditch' and 'brother'.

Brogan
Irish, meaning 'sturdy shoe'.

Bronwyn
Welsh, meaning 'white breasted'.

Brook
English, meaning 'stream'.

Bruce
Scottish, meaning 'high' or 'noble'.

Bruno
Germanic, meaning 'brown'.

Brewster
(alt. Brutus)
Latin, meaning 'dim-wit'.
The name of Julius Caesar's assassin.

B

Bryant
English variant of Brian, meaning 'high' or 'noble'.

Bryce
Scottish, meaning 'of Britain'.

Brycen
Scottish, meaning 'son of Bryce'.

Bryden
Irish, meaning 'strong one'.

Bryson
Welsh, meaning 'descendant of Brice'.

Bubba
American, meaning 'boy'.

Buck
American, meaning 'goat' or 'deer'.

Bud
(alt. Buddy)
American, meaning 'friend'.

Burdett
Middle English, meaning 'bird'.

Burgess
(alt. Burges, Burgiss, Berje)
English, meaning 'business'.

Burke
French, meaning 'fortified settlement'.

Burl
French, meaning 'knotty wood'.

Buzz
American, shortened form of Busby. Associated with the astronaut Buzz Aldrin.

Byron
Old English, meaning 'barn'. Made famous by the poet Lord Byron.

Sci-fi names
Anakin
Balin
Chike
Dante
Faizah
Fola
Hahzara
Kanene
Kibo
Shatea
Umi

C Boys' names

Cabot

Old English, meaning 'to sail'.

Cadby
(alt. Cadbey, Cadbee, Cadbie)
English, meaning 'soldier's colony'.

Cade
(alt. Caden)
English, meaning 'round/lumpy'.

Cadence

Latin, meaning 'with rhythm'.

Cadogan

Welsh, meaning 'battle glory and honour'.

Caedmon

Celtic, meaning 'wise warrior'.

Caelan

Gaelic, from St Columba.

Caerwyn
(alt. Carwyn, Gerwyn)
Welsh, meaning 'white fort' or 'settlement'.

Caesar

Latin, meaning 'head of hair'. Made famous by the first Roman emperor Julius Caesar.

Caetano

Portuguese, meaning 'from Gaeta, Italy'

Cagney

Irish, meaning 'successor of the advocate'.

C

Caiden
Arabic, meaning 'companion'.

Caillou
French, meaning 'pebble'.

Cain
Biblical, brother of Abel.

Cainan
Biblical, meaning 'possessor' or 'purchaser'.

Cairo
Egyptian city.

Cal
Short form of names beginning Cal-.

Calder
Scottish, meaning 'rough waters'.

Caleb
Hebrew, meaning 'dog'.

Calen
From Caleb, meaning 'dog'.

Calhoun
Irish, meaning 'slight woods'.

Calix
Greek, meaning 'very handsome'.

Callahan
Irish, meaning 'contention' or 'strife'.

Callum
Gaelic, meaning 'dove'.

Calvin
French, meaning 'little bald one'.

Camden
Gaelic, meaning 'winding valley'. Also an area of north London.

Cameron
Scottish Gaelic, meaning 'crooked nose'.

Camillo
Latin, meaning 'free born' or 'noble'.

Campbell
Scottish Gaelic, meaning 'crooked mouth'.

C

Canaan

Biblical, meaning 'to be humbled'.

Candido

Latin, meaning 'candid' or 'honest'.

Cannon

French, meaning 'of the church'.

Canton

French, 'dweller of corner'. Also name given to areas of Switzerland.

Canute
(alt. Cnut, Cnute)
Scandinavian, meaning 'knot'. Name of the King of England in the 11th century.

Cappy

Italian, meaning 'lucky'.

Carden

Old English, meaning 'wool carder'.

Carey

Gaelic, meaning 'love'.

Carl

Old Norse, meaning 'free man'.

Carlo

Italian form of Carl, meaning 'free man'.

Carlos

Spanish form of Carl, meaning 'free man'.

Carlton

Old English, meaning 'free peasant settlement'.

Carmelo

Latin, meaning 'garden' or 'orchard'.

Carmen

Latin/Spanish, meaning 'song'.

Carmine

Latin, meaning 'song'.

Carnell

English, meaning 'defender of the castle'.

Carson
(alt. Carsten)
Scottish, meaning 'marsh-dwellers'.

C

Carter
Old English, meaning 'transporter of goods'.

Cary
Old Celtic river name. Also means 'love'.

Case
(alt. Casey)
Irish Gaelic, meaning 'alert' or 'watchful'.

Cash
Latin, shortened form of Cassius, meaning 'vain'.

Casimer
Slavic, meaning 'famous destroyer of peace'.

Cason
Latin, from Cassius, meaning 'empty' or 'hollow'.

Casper
Persian, meaning 'treasurer'.

Caspian
From the Caspian Sea.

Cassidy
Gaelic, meaning 'curly haired'.

Cassius
(alt. Cassio)
Latin, meaning 'empty, hollow'.

Cathal
Celtic, meaning 'battle rule'.

TV personality names

Ant/hony (McPartlin)
Bruce (Forsyth)
Chris (Evans)
David (Dimbleby)
Dec/Ian (Donnelly)
Graham (Norton)
Jeremy (Clarkson, Kyle, Paxman)
Melvyn (Bragg)
Phillip (Schofield)
Simon (Cowell)

C

Cato
Latin, meaning 'all-knowing'.

Cecil
Latin, meaning 'blind'.

Cedar
English name of evergreen trees.

Cedric
Welsh, meaning 'spectacular bounty'.

Celestino
Spanish/Italian, meaning 'heavenly'.

Celesto
(alt. Celindo)
Latin, meaning 'heaven sent'.

Chad
(alt. Chadrick)
Old English, meaning 'warlike, warrior'.

Chaim
Hebrew, meaning 'life'.

Champion
English, from the word 'champion'.

Chance
English, from the word 'chance'.

Chandler
Old English, meaning 'candle maker and seller'.

Charles
(alt. Charlie)
Old German, meaning 'free man'.

Chaska
Native American name usually given to first son.

Che
Spanish, shortened form of Jose. Made famous by Che Guevara.

Chesley
Old English, meaning 'camp on the meadow'.

Chester
Latin, meaning 'camp of soldiers'.

Chilton
(alt. Chillron, Chilly, Chilt)
English, meaning 'tranquil'.

C

Chima
Old English, meaning 'hilly land'.

Christian
English, from the word Christian.

Christophe
French variant of Christopher, meaning 'bearing Christ inside'.

Christopher
Greek, meaning 'bearing Christ inside'.

Cian
Irish, meaning 'ancient'.

Ciaran
Irish, meaning 'black'.

Cicero
Latin, meaning 'chickpea'. Famous Roman philosopher and orator.

Cimarron
City in western Kansas.

Ciprian
Latin, meaning 'from Cyprus'.

Ciro
Spanish, meaning 'sun'.

Clancy
Old Irish, meaning 'red warrior'.

Clarence
Latin, meaning 'one who lives near the river Clare'.

Clark
Latin, meaning 'clerk'.

Claude
(alt. Claudie, Claudio, Claudius)
Latin, meaning 'lame'.

Claus
Variant of Nicholas, meaning 'people of victory'.

Clay
English, from the word 'clay'.

Clement
(alt. Clem)
Latin, meaning 'merciful'.

Cleo
Greek, meaning 'glory'.

C

Cletus
Greek, meaning 'illustrious'.

Cliff
(alt. Clifford, Clifton)
English, from the word 'cliff'.

Clint
(alt. Clinton)
Old English, meaning 'fenced settlement'.

Clive
English, meaning 'cliff'.

Clyde
Scottish, from the river in Glasgow.

Coby
(alt. Cody, Colby)
Irish, son of Oda.

Colden
Old English, meaning 'dark valley'.

Cole
Old French, meaning 'coal black'.

Coley
Old English, meaning 'coal black'.

Colin
Gaelic, meaning 'young creature'.

Colson
Old English, meaning 'coal black'.

Colton
English, meaning 'swarthy'.

Columbus
Latin, meaning 'dove'.

Colwyn
Welsh place name.

Conan
Gaelic, meaning 'wolf'.

Conley
Gaelic, meaning 'sensible'.

Connell
(alt. Connolly)
Irish, meaning 'high' or 'mighty'.

C

Connor
(alt. Conrad, Conroy)

Irish, meaning 'lover of hounds'.

Constant
(alt. Constantine)

English, from the word 'constant'.

Cooper

Old English, meaning 'barrel maker'.

Corban

Hebrew, meaning 'dedicated and belonging to God'.

Corbett
(alt. Corbin, Corby)

Norman French, meaning 'young crow'.

Cordell

Old English, meaning 'cord maker'.

Corey
(alt. Cory)

Gaelic, meaning 'hill hollow'.

Corin

Latin, meaning 'spear'.

Corliss
(alt. Corlis, Corlyss, Corlys)

English, meaning 'benevolent'.

Cormac

Gaelic, meaning 'impure son'.

Cornelius
(alt. Cornell)

Latin, meaning 'horn'.

Uncommon three-syllable names

Alastair
Barnaby
Dominic
Dorian
Elijah
Elliot
Lancelot
Roberto
Theodore

C

Cortez

Spanish, meaning 'courteous'.

Corwin

Old English, meaning 'heart's friend' or 'companion'.

Cosimo

(alt. Cosme, Cosmo)

Italian, meaning 'order' or 'beauty'.

Coty

French, meaning 'riverbank'.

Coulter

English, meaning 'young horse'.

Courtney

Old English, meaning 'domain of Curtis'.

Cowan

Gaelic, meaning 'hollow in the hill'.

Craig

Welsh, meaning 'rock'.

Crispin

Latin, meaning 'curly haired'.

Croix

French, meaning 'cross'.

Cruz

Spanish, meaning 'cross'. Made famous by David and Victoria Beckham's son.

Curran

Gaelic, meaning 'dagger' or 'hero'.

Curtis

(alt. Curt)

Old French, meaning 'courteous'.

Cutler

Old English, meaning 'knife maker'.

Cyprian

English, meaning 'from Cyprus'.

Cyril

Greek, meaning 'master' or 'Lord'.

Cyrus

Persian, meaning 'Lord'.

C

Popular American names for boys and girls

Arjay
Biff
Cooper
Jayson
Kayla
Keisha
Lacey
Landon
Phylician
Shequille

D

Boys' names

Dabeel
(*alt. Dabee, Dabie, Daby*)
Indian, meaning 'warrior'.

Dafydd
Welsh, meaning 'beloved'.
Made famous by the character
in the BBC television series
Little Britain.

Daichi
Japanese, meaning 'great
wisdom'.

Daire
(*alt. Daer, Daere, Dair*)
Irish, meaning 'wealthy'.

Daisuke
Japanese, meaning
'lionhearted'.

Dakari
African, meaning 'happy'.

Dale
Old English, meaning 'valley'.

Dallin
English, meaning 'dweller in the
valley'.

Dalton
English, meaning 'town in the
valley'.

Daly
Gaelic, meaning 'assembly'.

Damarion
Greek, meaning 'gentle'.

D

Damian
(alt. Damon)
Greek, meaning 'to tame/subdue'.

Dane
Old English, meaning 'from Denmark'.

Daniel
(alt. Dan, Danny)
Hebrew, meaning 'God is my judge'.

Dante
Latin, meaning 'lasting'. Associated with the Italian 13th century poet Dante Alighieri author of *The Divine Comdey*.

Darby
Irish, meaning 'without envy'.

Darcy
Gaelic, meaning 'dark'. Associated with Jane Austen's Mr Darcy, and the parody of this character in *Bridget Jones' Diary*.

Dario
(alt. Darius)
Greek, meaning 'kingly'.

Darnell
Old English, meaning 'the hidden spot'.

Darragh
Irish, meaning 'dark oak'.

Darrell
(alt. Daryl)
Old English, meaning 'open'.

Darren
(alt. Darrian)
Gaelic, meaning 'great'.

Darrick
Old German, meaning 'power of the tribe'.

Darshan
Hindi, meaning 'vision'.

Darwin
Old English, meaning 'dear friend'. Often associated with the naturalist Charles Darwin.

Dason
Native American, meaning 'chief'.

D

Dash
(alt. Dashawn)

American, meaning 'enlightened one'.

Dashiell
French, meaning 'page boy'.

David
(alt. Dave, Davey, Davie, Davian)

Biblical, meaning 'beloved'.

Davis
Old English, meaning 'son of David'.

Dawson
Old English, meaning 'son of David'.

Dax
(alt. Daxton)

French origin, was once a town in southwestern France. Now associated with the *Star Trek* character.

Dayal
Indian, meaning 'kind'.

Dayton
Old English, meaning 'David's place'.

Dean
Old English, meaning 'valley'.

Declan
Irish, meaning 'full of goodness'.

Dedric
Old English, meaning 'gifted ruler'.

Deepak
(alt. Deepan)

Indian, meaning 'illumination'.

Del
(alt. Delano, Delbert, Dell)

Old English, meaning 'bright shining one'.

Delaney
Irish, meaning 'dark challenge'.

Demetrius
Greek, meaning 'harvest lover'.

Dempsey
Irish, meaning 'proud'.

Denham
(alt. Denholm)

Old English, meaning 'valley settlement'.

D

Old name, new fashion?

Bertrand
Dexter
Felix
Hector
Jefferson
Norris
Pierce
Reginald
Ulysses
Winston

Dennis
(alt. Denny, Denton)

English, meaning 'follower of Dionysius'.

Denver

City in Colorado, USA.

Denzil
(alt. Denzel)

English, meaning 'fort'.

Deon

Greek, meaning 'of Zeus'.

Derek

English, meaning 'power of the tribe'.

Dermot

Irish, meaning 'free man'.

Desmond

Irish, meaning 'from south Munster'.

Destin

French, meaning 'destiny'.

Devyn

Irish, meaning 'poet'.

Dewey

Welsh origin, from Dewi (David).

Dexter
(alt. Dex)

Latin, meaning 'right-handed'.

Diallo
(alt. Dialo)

African, meaning 'bold'.

Dick
(alt. Dickie, Dickon)

From Richard, meaning 'powerful leader'.

Didier

French, meaning 'much desired'.

D

Diego

Spanish, meaning 'supplanter'.

Dietrich

Old German, meaning 'power of the tribe'.

Diggory

English, meaning 'dyke'.

Dilbert

English, meaning 'day-bright'.

Dimitri

(alt. Dimitrios, Dimitris)

Greek, meaning 'Prince'.

Dino

Diminutive of Dean, meaning 'valley'.

Dion

Greek, short form of Dionysius, the Greek god of wine.

Dirk

Variant of Derek, meaning 'power of the tribe'.

Divakar

Sanskrit, meaning 'the sun'.

Dobbin

Diminutive of Robert, meaning 'bright fame'.

Dominic

Latin, meaning 'Lord'.

Donald

(alt. Don, Donal, Donaldo)

Gaelic, meaning 'great chief'.

Donato

Italian, meaning 'gift'.

Donnell

(alt. Donnie, Donny)

Gaelic, meaning 'world fighter'.

Donovan

Gaelic, meaning 'dark-haired chief'.

Doran

Gaelic, meaning 'exile'.

Dorian

Greek, meaning 'descendant of Doris'. Name of the title character in Oscar Wilde's *The Picutre of Dorian Gray*.

Dorsey

From the French d'Orsay.

D

Douglas
(alt. Dougal, Dougie)
Scottish, meaning 'black river'.

Doyle
Irish, meaning 'foreigner'.

Draco
Latin, meaning 'dragon'. Made popular by the character Draco Malfoy in the *Harry Potter* novels.

Drake
Greek origin, meaning 'dragon'.

Drew
Shortened form of Andrew, meaning 'man' or 'warrior'.

Dryden
English, meaning 'dry town'.

Dudley
Old English, meaning 'people's field'. Also a town in the West Midlands, and the name of Harry Potter's cousin.

Duff
Gaelic, meaning 'swarthy'.

Duke
Latin origin, meaning 'leader'.

Duncan
Scottish, meaning 'dark warrior'.

Dustin
(alt. Dusty)
French origin, meaning 'brave warrior'.

Dwayne
Irish Gaelic origin, meaning 'swarthy'.

Dwight
Flemish, meaning 'blond'.

Dwyer
Gaelic, meaning 'dark wise one'.

Dyani
Native American, meaning 'eagle'.

Dylan
(alt. Dillon)
Welsh, meaning 'son of the sea'.

E

Boys' names

Eagan

Irish, meaning 'fiery'.

Eamon
(alt. Eames)

Irish, meaning 'wealthy protector'.

Earl
(alt. Earle, Errol)

English, from the word 'earl'.

Ebb

Short form of Ebenezer, meaning 'stone of help'.

Ebenezer

Hebrew, meaning 'stone of help'.

Ed
(alt. Edd, Eddie, Eddy)

Shortened form of Edward, meaning 'wealthy guard'.

Edgar
(alt. Elgar)

Old English, meaning 'wealthy spear'.

Edison

English, meaning 'son of Edward'.

Edmund

English, meaning 'wealthy protector'.

Edric

Old English, meaning 'rich and powerful'.

Edsel

Old German, meaning 'noble'.

Edward
(alt. Eduardo)

Old English, meaning 'wealthy guard'.

E

Edwin
English, meaning 'wealthy friend'.

Efrain
Hebrew, meaning 'fruitful'.

Egan
Irish, meaning 'fire'.

Eilif
(alt. Elif, Eilyg, Elyf)
Norse, meaning 'immortal'.

Einar
Old Norse, meaning 'battle leader'.

Eladio
Greek, meaning 'Greek'.

Elam
Hebrew, meaning 'eternal'.

Elbert
Old English, meaning 'famous'.

Eldon
Old English, meaning 'Ella's hill'.

Eldred
(alt. Eldridge)
Old English, meaning 'old venerable counsel'.

Elgin
Old English, meaning 'high minded'.

Eli
(alt. Eliah)
Hebrew, meaning 'high'.

Elias
(alt. Elijah)
Hebrew, meaning 'the Lord is my God'.

Elio
Spanish origin, meaning 'the Lord is my God'.

Ellery
Old English, meaning 'elder tree'.

Elliott
Variant of Elio, meaning 'the Lord is my God'.

Ellis
Welsh variant of Elio, meaning 'the Lord is my God'.

E

Ellison
English, meaning 'son of Ellis'.

Elmer
(alt. Elmo)
Old English, meaning 'noble'.

Elmo
(alt. Ellmo, Elmon)
Greek, meaning 'gregarious'. One of the characters in the children's television series *Sesame Street*.

Elon
Hebrew, meaning 'oak tree'.

Elroy
French, meaning 'king'.

Elton
Old English, meaning 'Ella's town'.

Elvin
English, meaning 'elf-like'.

Elvis
Figure in Norse mythology. Made famous by the singer Elvis Presley.

Emanuel
Hebrew, meaning 'God is with us'.

Emeric
German, meaning 'work rule'.

Emile
(alt. Emiliano, Emilio)
Latin, meaning 'eager'.

Emlyn
Welsh, name of town, Newcastle Emlyn, in West Wales.

Emmett
English origin, meaning 'universal'.

Emrys
Welsh, meaning 'immortal'.

Eneco
Spanish, meaning 'fiery one'.

Enoch
Hebrew, meaning 'dedicated'.

Enrico
(alt. Enrique)
Form of Henry, meaning 'home ruler'.

Enzo
Italian, short for Lorenzo, meaning 'laurel'.

E

Eoghan
(alt. Eoin)
Irish form of Owen, meaning 'well born' or 'noble'.

Eoin
Irish, meaning 'God is gracious'.

Ephron
(alt. Effron)
Biblical, meaning 'dust'.

Erasmo
(alt. Erasmus)
Greek, meaning 'to love'.

Eric
Old Norse, meaning 'ruler'.

Ernest
(alt. Ernesto, Ernie, Ernst)
Old German, meaning 'serious'.

Errol
English, meaning 'boar wolf'.

Erskine
Scottish, meaning 'high cliff'. Also a place in Scotland.

Erwin
Old English, meaning 'boar friend'.

Eryx
Greek, meaning 'boxer'.

Ethan
(alt. Etienne)
Hebrew, meaning 'long lived'.

Eugene
Greek, meaning 'well-born'.

Evan
Welsh, meaning 'God is good'.

Everard
Old English, meaning 'strong boar'.

Everett
English, meaning 'strong boar'.

Ewald
(alt. Ewan, Ewell)
From Owen, meaning 'well born' or 'noble'.

Ezra
Hebrew, meaning 'helper'. Associated with the poet Ezra Pound.

F

Boys' names

Faber
(alt. Fabir)
Latin, meaning 'blacksmith'.

Fabian
(alt. Fabien, Fabio)
Latin, meaning 'one who grows beans'.

Fabrice
(alt. Fabrizio)
Latin origin, meaning 'works with his hands'.

Faisal
Arabic, meaning 'resolute'.

Falco
(alt. Falcon, Falconer, Falke)
Latin meaning 'falconer'.

Faron
Spanish, meaning 'pharaoh'.

Farrell
Gaelic, meaning 'hero'.

Faulkner
Latin, from 'falcon'.

Faustino
Latin, meaning 'fortunate'.

Fela
(alt. Felah, Fella, Fellah)
African, meaning 'a man who is warlike'. The name of the famous Nigerian musician Fela Kuti.

F

Names of poets

Andrew (Marvell)
Geoffrey (Chaucer)
Hugo (Williams)
John (Donne, Keats, Milton)
Percy (Bysshe Shelley)
Robert (Burns)
Siegfried (Sassoon)
Ted (Hughes)
Walt (Whitman)
William (Blake, Wordsworth)

Felix
(alt. Felice)

Italian/Latin, meaning 'happy'.

Felipe
(alt. Filippo)

Spanish, meaning 'lover of horses'.

Fennel

Latin, name of a herb.

Ferdinand
(alt. Fernando)

Old German, meaning 'bold voyager'.

Fergus
(alt. Ferguson)

Gaelic, meaning 'supreme man'.

Ferris

Gaelic, meaning 'rock'.

Fiachra

Irish, meaning 'raven'.

Fidel

Latin, meaning 'faithful'.

Finbar

Gaelic, meaning 'fair head'.

Finian

Gaelic, meaning 'fair'.

F

Finlay
(alt. Finley, Finn)
Gaelic, meaning 'fair haired courageous one'.

Finnegan
Gaelic, meaning 'fair'.

Fintan
Gaelic, meaning 'little fair one'.

Fitzroy
English, meaning 'the king's son'.

Flavio
Latin, meaning 'yellow hair'.

Florencio
(alt. Florentino)
Latin, meaning 'from Florence'.

Florian
(alt. Florin)
Slavic/Latin, meaning 'flower'.

Floyd
Welsh origin, meaning 'grey haired'.

Flynn
Gaelic, meaning 'with a ruddy complexion'.

Forbes
(alt. Forbs, Forb, Forbe)
Gaelic, meaning 'of the field'.

Fortunato
Italian, meaning 'lucky'.

Foster
Old English, meaning 'woodsman'.

Fotini
(alt. Fotis)
Greek, meaning 'light'.

Francesco
(alt. Francis, Francisco, Franco, François)
Latin, meaning 'from France'.

Frank
(alt. Frankie, Franklin, Franz)
Middle English, meaning 'free landholder'.

Fraser
Scottish, meaning 'of the forest men'.

F

Fred
(alt. Freddie, Frederick)

Old German, meaning 'peaceful ruler'.

Fyfe
(alt. Fife, Fyffes)

Scottish, meaning 'from Fifeshire'.

Furman

Old German, meaning 'ferryman'.

Shakespearean names

Angelo (*Measure for Measure*)
Anthony (*Anthony and Cleopatra*)
Balthazar (*Romeo and Juliet*)
Hamlet (*Hamlet*)
Henry (*Henry V*)
Iago (*Othello*)
Othello (*Othello*)
Richard (*Richard III*)
Romeo (*Romeo and Juliet*)
Sebastian (*Twelfth Night*)

G

Boys' names

Gabe

Shortened form of Gabriel, meaning 'hero of God'.

Gabino

Latin origin, meaning 'God is my strength'.

Gabriel

Hebrew, meaning 'hero of God'. One of the archangels.

Gael

English, old reference to the Celts.

Gaetano

Italian, from Gaeto in central Italy.

Gaius
(alt. Gaeus)

Latin, meaning 'rejoicing'.

Galen

Greek origin, meaning 'healer'.

Galileo

Italian, meaning 'from Galilee'.

Ganesh

Hindi, meaning 'Lord of the throngs'. One of the Hindu deities.

Gannon

Irish, meaning 'fair skinned'.

Gareth
(alt. Garth)

Welsh, meaning 'gentle'.

G

Garfield

Old English, meaning 'spear field'. Also the name of the cartoon cat.

Garland

English, as in 'garland of flowers'.

Garnet

English, precious stone red in colour.

Garry
(alt. Gary, Geary)

Old English, meaning 'spear'.

Garth
(alt. Garthe, Gart, Garte)

Norse, meaning 'enclosure'.

Gaspar
(alt. Gaspard)

Persian, meaning 'treasurer'.

Gaston

From the Gascony region in the south of France.

Gavin
(alt. Gawain)

Scottish/Welsh, meaning 'little falcon'.

Gene

Shortened form of Eugene, meaning 'well born'.

Genkei

Japanese, meaning 'honoured'.

Gennaro

Italian, meaning 'of Janus'.

Geoffrey

Old German, meaning 'peace'.

George
(alt. Giorgio)

Greek, meaning 'farmer'.

Gerald
(alt. Geraldo, Gerard, Gerardo, Gerhard)

Old German, meaning 'spear ruler'.

Geronimo

Italian origin, meaning 'sacred name'.

Gerry

English, meaning 'independent'.

G

Gert

Old German, meaning 'strong spear'.

Gervase

Old German, meaning 'with honour'.

Giacomo

Italian, meaning 'God's son'.

Gibson

English, meaning 'son of Gilbert'.

Gideon

Hebrew, meaning 'tree cutter'.

Gilbert

(alt. Gilberto)

French, meaning 'bright promise'.

Giles

Greek, meaning 'small goat'.

Gino

Italian, meaning 'well born'.

Giovanni

Italian form of John, meaning 'God is gracious'.

Giri

(alt. Ririe, Giry, Girey)

Indian, meaning 'from the mountain'.

Giulio

Italian, meaning 'youthful'.

Giuseppe

Italian form of Joseph, meaning 'Jehovah increases'.

Glen

English, from the word 'glen'.

Glyn

Welsh form of Glen.

Godfrey

German, meaning 'peace of God'.

Gordon

Gaelic, meaning 'large fortification'.

Gottlieb

German, meaning 'good love'.

Gower

Area on the Welsh coast.

G

Graeme
(alt. Graham)
English, meaning 'gravelled area'.

Grant
English, from the word 'grant'.

Granville
English, meaning 'gravelly town'.

Gray
(alt. Grey)
English, from the word 'gray'.

Grayson
English, meaning 'son of gray'.

Green
English, from the word 'green'.

Greg
(alt. Gergorio, Gregory, Grieg)
English, meaning 'watcher'.

Griffin
English, from the word 'griffin'.

Groves
English, meaning 'inhabits near grove of trees'.

Guido
Italian, meaning 'guide'.

Guillaume
French form of William, meaning 'strong protector'.

Gulliver
English, meaning 'glutton'.

Gunther
German, meaning 'warrior'.

Gurpreet
Indian, meaning 'love of the teacher'.

Gustave
(alt. Gus)
Scandinavian, meaning 'royal staff'.

Guy
English, from the word 'guy'.

Grylfi
(alt. Gylfie, Gylfee, Gylffi)
Scandanavian, meaning 'king'.

Gwyn
Welsh, meaning 'white'.

H

Boys' names

Habib

Arabic, meaning 'beloved one'.

Hackett
(alt. Hacket, Hackit, Hackitt)

German, meaning 'small hacker'.

Haden
(alt. Haiden)

English, meaning 'hedged valley'.

Hades

Greek, meaning 'sightless'. Name of the underworld in Greek mythology.

Hadrian

From Hadria, a north Italian city.

Hadwin

Old English, meaning 'friend in war'.

Hakeem

Arabic, meaning 'wise and insightful'.

Hal
(alt. Hale, Hallie)

English, nickname for Henry, meaning 'home ruler'.

Halim

Arabic, meaning 'gentle'.

Hamid

Arabic, meaning 'praiseworthy'.

H

Hamilton

Old English, meaning 'flat topped hill'.

Hamish

Scottish form of James, meaning 'he who supplants'.

Hamlet

(alt. Hamlett, Hammet, Hamnet)

German, meaning 'village'. A variation of the Danish Amleth, and often associated with Shakespeare's tragedy *Hamlet*.

Hampus

Swedish form of Homer, meaning 'pledge'.

Hamza

Arabic, meaning 'lamb'.

Han

(alt. Hannes, Hans)

Scandinavian, meaning 'the Lord is gracious'.

Hanif

(alt. Haneef, Haneaf, Haneif)

Arabic, meaning 'devout'.

Hank

German, meaning 'home ruler'. Form of Henry.

Hansel

German, meaning 'the Lord is gracious'.

Hardy

English, meaning 'tough'. Often associated with the author Thomas Hardy.

Harlan

English, meaning 'dweller by the boundary wood'.

Names from ancient Greece

Aeschylus
Berenice
Erasmus
Hieronymus
Homer
Jason
Leonidas
Nikolaos
Sophocles
Theodore

H

Harland

Old English, meaning 'army land'.

Harley

Old English, meaning 'hare meadow'.

Harmon

Old German, meaning 'soldier'.

Harold

Scandinavian, meaning 'army ruler'.

Harry

Old German, meaning 'home ruler'. Form of Henry.

Hart

Old English, meaning 'stag'.

Harvey

Old English, meaning 'strong and worthy'.

Haskell

Hebrew, meaning 'intellect'.

Hassan

Arabic, meaning 'handsome'.

Haydn

Old English, meaning 'hedged valley'.

Heart

English, from the word 'heart'.

Heath

English, meaning 'heath' or 'moor'.

Heathcliff

English, meaning 'cliff near a heath'. Made famous by Emily Bronte's novel *Wuthering Heights*.

Heber

Hebrew, meaning 'partner'.

Hector

Greek, meaning 'steadfast'.

Henry

(alt. Henri, Hendrik, Hendrix)

Old German, meaning 'home ruler'.

Henson

English, meaning 'son of Henry'.

H

Herbert
(alt. Bert, Herb)
Old German, meaning 'illustrious warrior'.

Heriberto
Spanish variant of Herbert, meaning 'illustrious warrior'.

Herman
(alt. Herminio, Hermon)
Old German, meaning 'soldier'.

Hermes
Greek, meaning 'messenger'. The messenger of the gods in Greek mythology.

Herschel
Yiddish, meaning 'deer'.

Hezekiah
Biblical, meaning 'God gives strength'.

Hideki
Japanese, meaning 'excellent trees'.

Hideo
Japanese, meaning 'excellent name'.

Hilario
Latin, meaning 'cheerful, happy'.

Hilary
English, meaning 'cheerful'.

Hillel
Hebrew, meaning 'greatly praised'.

Hilliard
Old German, meaning 'battle guard'.

Hilton
Old English, meaning 'hill settlement'.

Hiram
Hebrew, meaning 'exalted brother'.

Hiro
From Spanish, meaning 'sacred name'.

Hiroshi
Japanese, meaning 'generous'.

Hirsch
Yiddish, meaning 'deer'.

H

Hobart

English, meaning 'bright and shining intellect'.

Hodge

English, meaning 'son of Roger'.

Hogan

Gaelic, meaning 'youth'.

Holden

English, meaning 'deep valley'.

Hollis

Old English, meaning 'holly tree'.

Homer

Greek, meaning 'pledge'. Name of the Greek poet and TV character Homer Simpson.

Honorius

Latin, meaning 'honourable'.

Horace

Latin, name of the Roman poet.

Houston

Old English, meaning 'Hugh's town'. Also city in the state of Texas, USA.

Howard

Old English, meaning 'noble watchman'.

Howell

Welsh, meaning 'eminent and remarkable'.

Hoyt

Norse, meaning 'spirit' or 'soul'.

Hristo

From Christo, meaning 'follower of Christ'.

Hubbell
(alt. Hubble)

English, meaning 'brave hearted'.

Hubert

German, meaning 'bright and shining intellect'.

Hudson

Old English, meaning 'son of Hugh'.

Hugh

Old German, meaning 'soul, mind and intellect'.

H

Hugo

German, meaning 'bright in mind and spirit'.

Humbert

Old German, meaning 'famous giant'. Be warned: it's the name and surname of the paedophile protagonist of Vladimir Nabokov's *Lolita*.

Humphrey

Old German, meaning 'peaceful warrior'.

Hunter

English, from the word 'hunter'.

Hurley

Gaelic, meaning 'sea tide'.

Huxley

Old English, meaning 'Hugh's meadow'.

Hyrum

Hebrew, meaning 'exalted brother'.

Surnames as first names

Campbell
Connor
Cooper
Hamilton
Harrison
Lewis
Jackson
Taylor
Walker
Watson

Boys' names

Iago

Spanish, meaning 'he who supplants'. Name of the villain in Shakespeare's *Othello*.

Ian
(alt. Ion)

Variant of John, meaning 'God is gracious'.

Ianto

Welsh, meaning 'gift of God'.

Ibaad

Arabic, meaning 'a believer in God'.

Ibrahim

Arabic, meaning 'father of many'.

Ichabod

Hebrew, meaning 'glory is good'.

Idan

Hebrew, meaning 'place in time'.

Ichiro

Japanese, meaning 'first born son'.

Idris

Welsh, meaning 'fiery leader'.

Ifan

Welsh variant of John, meaning 'God is gracious'.

I

Ignacio
Latin, meaning 'ardent' or 'burning'.

Ignatz
German, meaning 'fiery'.

Igor
Russian, meaning 'Ing's soldier'.

Ikaika
Hawaiian, meaning 'strong'.

Ike
Hebrew, short for Isaac, meaning 'laughter'.

Iku
Japanese, meaning 'nourishing'.

Ilan
Hebrew, meaning 'tree'.

Ilias
Variant of Hebrew Elijah, meaning 'the Lord is my God'.

Imanol
Hebrew, meaning 'God is with us'.

Indiana
Latin, meaning 'from India'. Also a state in the US.

Indigo
English, describing a deep blue colour.

Ingo
Danish, meaning 'meadow'.

Inigo
Spanish, meaning 'fiery'.

Ioannis
Greek, meaning 'the Lord is gracious'.

Girls' names for boys (male spellings)

Darcy
Jean
Kay
Kelly
Kelsey
Madison
Nat
Paris
Sandy
Sasha

Iovianno

Native American, meaning 'yellow hawk'.

Ira

Hebrew, meaning 'full grown and watchful'.

Irvin
(alt. Irving, Irwin)

Gaelic, meaning 'green and fresh water'.

Isaac
(alt. Isaak)

Hebrew, meaning 'laughter'.

Isadore
(alt. Isidore, Isidro)

Greek, meaning 'gift of Isis'.

Isai
(alt. Isaiah, Isaias, Izaiah)

Arabic, meaning 'protection and security'.

Iser

Yiddish, meaning 'God wrestler'.

Ishedus

Native American, meaning 'on top'.

Place names

Austin
Carson
Chester
Glen
Jericho
London
Paris
Seymour
Whitley
Windsor

Ishmael
(alt. Ismael)

Hebrew, meaning 'God listens'.

Israel

Hebrew, meaning 'God perseveres'. Also the name of the country.

Istvan

Hungarian variant of Stephen, meaning 'crowned'.

Itai

Hebrew, meaning 'the Lord is with me'.

I

Ivan

Hebrew, meaning 'God is gracious'.

Ivanhoe

Russian origin, meaning 'God is gracious'. Also name of the novel by Walter Scott.

Ivey

English, variant of Ivy.

Ivo

From the French 'yves', meaning 'yew tree'.

Ivor

Scandinavian, meaning 'yew'.

Ivory

English, from the word 'ivory'.

Izar

Basque, meaning 'star'.

Long names

Alexander
Bartholomew
Christopher
Demetrius
Giovanni
Montgomery
Obadiah
Roberto
Salvatore
Zachariah

J Boys' names

Jabari
Swahili, meaning 'valiant'.

Jabez
Hebrew, meaning 'borne in pain'.

Jabulani
(alt. Jabulanie, Jabulany, Jabulaney)
African, meaning 'happy one'.

Jace
(alt. Jaece, Jase, Jayce)
Hebrew, meaning 'healer'.

Jacek
African, meaning 'hyacinth'.

Jacinto
African, meaning 'hyacinth'.

Jack
(alt. Jackie, Jacky)
From the Hebrew John, meaning 'God is gracious'.

Jackson
English, meaning 'son of Jack'.

Jaco
From the Hebrew Jacob, meaning 'he who supplants'.

Jacob
(alt. Jacobo, Jago)
Hebrew, meaning 'he who supplants'.

Jacques
French form of Jack, meaning 'God is gracious'.

J

Jaden
(alt. Jaden, Jadyn, Jaeden, Jaiden, Jaidyn, Jayden, Jaydin)
Hebrew, meaning 'Jehovah has heard'.

Jaegar
(alt. Jager, Jaecer, Jaegar)
German, meaning 'mighty hunter'.

Jafar
Arabic, meaning 'stream'.

Jagger
Old English, meaning 'one who cuts'.

Jaheem
(alt. Jaheim)
Hebrew, meaning 'raised up'.

Jahir
Hindi, meaning 'jewel'.

Jaime
Variant for James, meaning 'he who supplants'. 'J'aime' is French for 'I love'.

Jair
(alt. Jairo)
Hebrew, meaning 'God enlightens'.

Jake
Shortened form of Jacob, meaning 'he who supplants'.

Jalen
Greek, meaning 'healer' or 'tranquil'.

Jali
Swahili, meaning 'musician'.

Jalon
Greek, meaning 'healer' or 'tranquil'.

Jamaal
(alt. Jamal)
Arabic, meaning 'handsome'.

Jamar
(alt. Jamarcus, Jamari, Jamarion, Jamir)
Modern variant of Jamal, meaning 'handsome'.

Jamel
Arabic, meaning 'handsome'.

James

English, meaning 'he who supplants'.

Jameson
(alt. Jamison)

English, meaning 'son of James'.

Jamie
(alt. Jamey, Jaimie)

Nickname for James, meaning 'he who supplants'.

Jamil

Arabic, meaning 'handsome'.

Jamin

Hebrew, meaning 'son of the right hand'.

Jan
(alt. Janko, János)

Slavic, from John meaning 'the Lord is gracious'.

Janesh

Hindi, meaning 'leader of people'.

Janus

Latin, meaning 'gateway'. Roman god of doors, beginnings and endings.

Japhet
(alt. Japheth)

Hebrew, meaning 'comely'.

Jaquez

French origin, form of Jacques, meaning 'God is gracious'.

Jared
(alt. Jarem, Jaren, Jaret, Jarod, Jarrod)

Hebrew, meaning 'descending'.

Short names

Al
Ben
Dev
Ed
Jo
Kev
Max
Rob
Sam
Ty

J

Jarlath

Gaelic, from Iarlaith, from Saint Iarfhlaith.

Jarom

Greek, meaning 'to raise and exalt'.

Jarrell

Variant of Gerald, meaning 'spear ruler'.

Jarrett

Old English, meaning 'spear-brave'.

Jarvis

Old German, meaning 'with honour'.

Jason

Greek, meaning 'healer'.

Jasper

Greek, meaning 'treasure holder'.

Javen

Arabic, meaning 'youth'.

Javier

Spanish, meaning 'bright'.

Jaxon

From Jackson, meaning 'son of Jack'.

Jay

Latin, meaning 'jaybird'.

Jaylan

Greek, meaning 'healer'.

Jeevan

Indian, meaning 'life'.

Jefferey
(alt. Jeff)

Old German, meaning 'peace'.

Jefferson

English, meaning 'son of Jeffrey'.

Jensen

Scandinavian, meaning 'son of Jan'.

Jeremiah
(alt. Jeremia, Jeremias, Jeremiya)

Hebrew, meaning 'the Lord exalts'.

J

Jeremy
(alt. Jem)

Hebrew, meaning 'the Lord exalts'.

Jeriah

Hebrew, meaning 'Jehovah has seen'.

Jericho

Arabic, meaning 'city of the moon'.

Jermaine

Latin, meaning 'brotherly'.

Jerome

Greek, meaning 'sacred name'.

Jerry

English, from Gerald, meaning 'spear ruler'.

Jesse

Hebrew, meaning 'the Lord exists'.

Jesus

Hebrew, meaning 'the Lord is Salvation' and the Son of God.

Jethro

Hebrew, meaning 'eminent'.

Jignesh
(alt. Jigneshe, Jygnesh, Jygneshe)

Indian, meaning 'curious'.

Jim
(alt. Jimmy)

From James, meaning 'he who supplants'.

Jiri
(alt. Jiro)

Greek, meaning 'farmer'.

Joachim

Hebrew, meaning 'established by God'.

Joah
(alt. João)

Hebrew, meaning 'God is gracious'.

Joaquin

Hebrew, meaning 'established by God'. Made famous by the actor Joaquin Phoenix.

J

Joe
(alt. Joey, Johan, Johannes, Jomar)
From Joseph, meaning 'Jehovah increases'.

Joel
Hebrew, meaning 'Jehovah is the Lord'.

John
Hebrew, meaning 'the Lord is gracious'.

Johnny
(alt. Jon, Jonny)
From Jonathan, meaning 'gift of God'.

Jolyon
From Julian, meaning 'young'.

Jonah
Hebrew, meaning 'dove'.

Jonas
Hebrew, meaning 'dove'.

Jonathan
(alt. Johnathan, Johnathon, Jonathon, Jonty)
Hebrew, meaning 'gift from God'.

Jordan
(alt. Jory, Judd)
Hebrew, meaning 'down-flowing'.

Jorge
From George, meaning 'farmer'.

José
Spanish variant of Joseph, meaning 'Jehovah increases'.

Joseph
(alt. Joss)
Hebrew, meaning 'Jehovah increases'.

Josh
Shortened form of Joshua, meaning 'Jehovah is salvation'.

Joshua
Hebrew, meaning 'Jehovah is salvation'.

Josiah
Hebrew, meaning 'Jehovah helps'.

Josué
Spanish variant of Joshua, meaning 'Jehovah is salvation'.

J

'Bad boy' names

Arnie
Axel
Brett
Conan
Damian
Guy
Ivan
Preston
Stanley
Tyson

Jovan

Latin, meaning 'the supreme God'.

Joweese

Native American, meaning 'chirping bird'.

Joyce

Latin, meaning 'joy'.

Juan

Spanish variant of John, meaning 'the Lord is gracious'.

Jubal

Hebrew, meaning 'ram's horn'.

Jude

Hebrew, meaning 'praise' or 'thanks'. The title character in Hardy's novel *Jude the Obscure*.

Judson

Variant of Jude, meaning 'praise' or 'thanks'.

Jules

From Julian, meaning 'Jove's child'.

Julian

Greek, meaning 'Jove's child'.

Julien

French variant of Julian, meaning 'Jove's child'.

Julio

Spanish variant of Julian, meaning 'Jove's child'.

Julius

Latin, meaning 'youthful'.

Junior

Latin, meaning 'the younger one'.

J

Junius
Latin, meaning 'young'.

Jupiter
Latin, meaning 'the supreme God'. Jupiter was king of the Roman gods and the god of thunder. Jupiter is also the largest planet in the solar system.

Juraj
Hebrew, meaning 'God is my judge'.

Jurgen
Greek, meaning 'farmer'.

Justice
English, from the word 'justice'.

Justin
(alt. Justus)

Latin, meaning 'just and upright'.

Juwan
Hebrew, meaning 'the Lord is gracious'.

Famous male drummers

Dave (Grohl)
John (Bonham)
Keith (Moon)
Lars (Ulrich)
Mick (Fleetwood)
Phil (Collins)
Ringo (Starr)
Stewart (Copeland)
Tommy (Lee)
Travis (Barker)

K Boys' names

Kaamil

Arabic, meaning 'perfect'.

Kabelo

African, meaning 'gift'.

Kade

Scottish, meaning 'from the wetlands'.

Kadeem

Arabic, meaning 'one who serves'.

Kaden

(alt. *Kadin, Kaeden, Kaedin, Kaiden*)

Arabic, meaning 'companion'.

Kadir

Arabic, meaning 'capable and competent'.

Kafka

Czech, meaning 'bird-like'. Often associated with the author of *The Metamorphosis*.

Kahlil

Arabic, meaning 'friend'.

Kai

Greek, meaning 'keeper of the keys'.

Kaito

Japanese, meaning 'ocean and sake dipper'.

K

Kalani
Hawaiian, meaning 'sky'.

Kale
German, meaning 'free man'.

Kaleb
Hebrew, meaning 'dog' or 'aggressive'.

Kalen
Gaelic, meaning 'uncertain'.

Kaleo
Hawaiian, meaning 'the voice'.

Kalil
Arabic, meaning 'friend'.

Kalvin
French, meaning 'bald'.

Kamari
Indian, meaning 'the enemy of desire'.

Kamden
English, meaning 'winding valley'.

Kamil
Arabic, meaning 'perfection'.

Kane
Gaelic, meaning 'little battler'.

Kani
Hawaiian, meaning 'sound'.

Kanye
African town. Made popular by rapper Kanye West.

Kareem
(alt. Karim)
Arabic, meaning 'generous'.

Karl
(alt. Karson)
Old German, meaning 'free man'.

Kasey
Irish, meaning 'alert'.

Kaspar
Persian, meaning 'treasurer'.

Kavon
Gaelic, meaning 'handsome'.

Kayden

Arabic, meaning 'companion'.

Kazimierz

Polish, meaning 'declares peace'.

Kazuki

Japanese, meaning 'radiant hope'.

Kazuo

Japanese, meaning 'harmonious man'.

Keagan
(alt. Keegan, Kegan)

Gaelic, meaning 'small flame'.

Keane

Gaelic, meaning 'fighter'.

Keanu

Hawaiian, meaning 'breeze'. Made famous by the actor Keanu Reeves.

Keary

Gaelic, meaning 'black-haired'.

Keaton

English, meaning 'place of hawks'.

Keefe
(alt. Keef, Kief, Kiefe)

Gaelic, meaning 'beautiful and graceful'.

Keeler

Gaelic, meaning 'beautiful and graceful'.

Keenan
(alt. Kenan)

Gaelic, meaning 'little ancient one'.

Keiji

Japanese, meaning 'govern with discretion'.

Keir

Gaelic, meaning 'dark-haired' or 'dark-skinned'.

Keith

Gaelic, meaning 'woodland'.

Kekoa

Hawaiian, meaning 'brave one' or 'soldier'.

Kelby

Old English, meaning 'farmhouse near the stream'.

K

K

Kell

(alt. Kellan, Kellen, Kelley, Kelly, Kiel)

Norse, meaning 'spring'.

Kelsey

Old English, meaning 'victorious ship'.

Kelton

Old English, meaning 'town of the keels'.

Kelvin

Old English, meaning 'friend of ships'.

Kemenes

Hungarian, meaning 'maker of furnaces'.

Ken

Shortened form of Kenneth, meaning 'born of fire'.

Kendal

Old English, meaning 'the Kent river valley'.

Kendon

Old English, meaning 'brave guard'.

Kendrick

Gaelic, meaning 'royal ruler'.

Kenelm

Old English, meaning 'bold'.

Kenji

Japanese, meaning 'intelligent second son'.

Kennedy

Gaelic, meaning 'helmet head'.

Kenneth

(alt. Kenney)

Gaelic, meaning 'born of fire'.

Kennison

English, meaning 'son of Kenneth'.

Kent

From the English county.

Kenton

English, meaning 'town of Ken'.

Kenya

From the country in Africa.

Kenzo

Japanese, meaning 'wise'.

K

Keola

Hawaiian, meaning 'life'.

Keon
(*alt. Keoni*)

Hawaiian, meaning 'gracious'.

Kepler

German, meaning 'hat maker'.

Kermit
(*alt. Kerwin*)

Gaelic, meaning 'without envy'. Associated with Kermit the Frog, the Muppets character.

Kerr

English, meaning 'wetland'.

Keshav

Indian, meaning 'beautiful-haired'.

Kevin

Gaelic, meaning 'handsome beloved'.

Khalid
(*alt. Khalif, Khalil*)

Arabic, meaning 'immortal'.

Kian
(*alt. Keyon, Kyan*)

Irish, meaning 'ancient'.

Kiefer

German, meaning 'barrel maker'.

Kieran
(*alt. Kyron*)

Gaelic, meaning 'black'.

Kijana

African, meaning 'youth'.

Kilby

From the English 'Cilebi', a place in Leicestershire.

Kilian

Irish, meaning 'bright headed'.

Kimani

African, meaning 'beautiful and sweet'.

King

English, from the word 'king'.

Kingsley

English, meaning 'the king's meadow'.

K

Kirby
German, meaning 'settlement by a church'.

Kirk
Old German, meaning 'church'.

Klaus
German, meaning 'victorious'.

Knightley
(alt. Knightly)
English, meaning 'of the knight's meadows'. Surname of the hero in Jane Austen's *Emma*.

Kobe
(alt. Koda, Kody)
Japanese, meaning 'a Japanese city'.

Kofi
Ghanaian, meaning 'born on Friday'.

Kohana
Japanese, meaning 'little flower'.

Kojo
Ghanaian, meaning 'Monday'.

Kolby
Norse, meaning 'settlement'.

Korbin
Gaelic, meaning 'a steep hill'.

Kramer
German, meaning 'shopkeeper'.

Kris
(alt. Krish)
From Christopher, meaning 'bearing Christ inside'.

Kurt
German, meaning 'courageous advice'.

Kurtis
French, meaning 'courtier'.

Kwame
Ghanaian, meaning 'born on Saturday'.

Kyden

English, meaning 'narrow little fire'.

Kylan
(alt. *Kyle, Kyleb, Kyler*)

Gaelic, meaning 'narrow and straight'.

Kyllion

Irish, meaning 'war'.

Kyree

From Cree, a Canadian tribe.

Kyros

Greek, meaning 'legitimate power'.

K

L Boys' names

Laban
Hebrew, meaning 'white'.

Lachlan
Gaelic, meaning 'from the land of lakes'.

Lacy
Old French place name.

Laertes
English, meaning 'adventurous'. Ophelia's brother in Shakespeare's *Hamlet*.

Lalit
Hindi, meaning 'beautiful'.

Lamar
Old German, meaning 'water'.

Lambert
Scandinavian, meaning 'land brilliant'.

Lambros
Greek, meaning 'brilliant and radiant'.

Lamont
Old Norse, meaning 'law man'.

Lance
French, meaning 'land'.

Lancelot
Variant of Lance, meaning 'land'. The name of one of the knights of the Round Table.

Landen
(*alt. Lando, Landon, Langdon*)
English, meaning 'long hill'.

L

Landyn
Welsh variant of Landen, meaning 'long hill'.

Lane
(alt. Layne)
English, from the word 'lanel'.

Lang
Norse, meaning 'long meadow'.

Lannie
(alt. Lanny)
German, meaning 'precious'.

Larkin
Gaelic, meaning 'rough' or 'fierce'.

Laron
French, meaning 'thief'.

Larry
French, meaning 'man from Laurentum'.

Lars
Scandinavian variant of Lawrence, meaning 'man from Laurentum'.

Lasse
Finnish, meaning 'girl'. (Still, ironically, a boy's name.)

Laszlo
Hungarian, meaning 'glorious rule'.

Lathyn
Latin, meaning 'fighter'.

Latif
Arabic, meaning 'gentle'.

Laurel
Latin, meaning 'bay'.

Laurent
French, from Lawrence, meaning 'man from Laurentum'.

Lawrence
Latin, meaning 'man from Laurentum'.

Lazarus
Hebrew, meaning 'God is my help'.

Leandro
Latin, meaning 'lion man'.

Lear

German, meaning 'of the meadow'.

Lee
(alt. Leigh)

Old English, meaning 'meadow' or 'valley'.

Leib

German, meaning 'love'.

Leif

Scandinavian, meaning 'heir'.

Leith

From the name of a place in Scotland.

Lennox
(alt. Lenny)

Gaelic, meaning 'with many elm trees'.

Leo

Latin, meaning 'lion'.

Leon

Latin, meaning 'lion'.

Leonard

Old German, meaning 'lion strength'.

Leopold

German, meaning 'brave people'.

Leroy

French, meaning 'king'.

Lesley
(alt. Les)

Scottish, meaning 'holly garden'.

Lester

English, meaning 'from Leicester'.

Lewis

French, meaning 'renowned fighter'.

Lex

English alternative of Alexander, meaning 'defending men'.

Liam

German, meaning 'helmet'.

Lincoln

English, meaning 'lake colony'.

Lindsay

Scottish, meaning 'linden tree'.

L

L

Linus

Latin, meaning 'lion'.

Lionel

English, meaning 'lion'.

Llewellyn

Welsh, meaning 'like a lion'.

Lloyd

Welsh, meaning 'grey-haired and sacred'.

Logan

Gaelic, meaning 'hollow'.

Lonnie

English, meaning 'lion strength'.

Lorcan

Gaelic, meaning 'little fierce one'.

Louis

(alt. Lou, Louie, Luigi, Luis)

German, meaning 'famous warrior'.

Lucas

(alt. Lukas)

English, meaning 'man from Luciana'.

Lucian

(alt. Lucio)

Latin, meaning 'light'.

Ludwig

German, meaning 'famous fighter'.

Luke

(alt. Luc, Luka)

Latin, meaning 'from Lucanus'.

Lupe

Latin, meaning 'wolf'.

Luther

German, meaning 'soldier of the people'.

Lyle

French, meaning 'the island'.

Lyn

(alt. Lyndon)

Spanish, meaning 'pretty'.

Boys' names

Mabon
(alt. Maban, Mabery)
Welsh, meaning 'our son'.

Mac
(alt. Mack, Mackie)
Scottish, meaning 'son of'.

Macaulay
Scottish, meaning 'son of the phantom'.

Mace
English, meaning 'heavy staff' or 'club'.

Mackenzie
Scottish, meaning 'the fair one'.

Mackland
Scottish, meaning 'land of Mac'.

Macon
French origin, name of towns in France and Georgia.

Macsen
Scottish, meaning 'son of Mac'.

Madden
Irish, meaning 'descendant of the hound'.

Maddox
English, meaning 'good' or 'generous'.

Madison
(alt. Madsen)
Irish, meaning 'son of Madden'.

Mads

Shortened form of Madden, meaning 'descendant of the hound'.

Magnus
(alt. Manus)
Latin, meaning 'great'.

Maguire

Gaelic, meaning 'son of the beige one'.

Mahesh

Hindi, meaning 'great ruler'.

Mahabala

Indian, meaning 'great strength'.

Mahir

Arabic, meaning 'skillful'.

Mahlon

Hebrew, meaning 'sickness'.

Mahmoud

Arabic, meaning 'praiseworthy'.

Mahoney

Irish, meaning 'bear'.

Major

English, from the word 'major'.

Makal

From Michael, meaning 'close to God'.

Makani

Hawaiian, meaning 'wind'.

Makis

Hebrew, meaning 'gift from God'.

Mako

Hebrew, meaning 'God is with us'.

Malachi
(alt. Malachy)
Irish, meaning 'messenger of God'.

Malcolm

English, meaning 'Columba's servant'.

Mali

Arabic, meaning 'full and rich'.

Manfred

Old German, meaning 'man of peace'.

Manish
English, meaning 'manly'.

Manley
English, meaning 'manly and brave'.

Mannix
Gaelic, meaning 'little monk'.

Manoi
(alt. Manos)
Japanese, meaning 'love springing from intellect'.

Manuel
Hebrew, meaning 'God is with us'.

Manzi
Italian, meaning 'steer'.

Marc
(alt. Marco, Marcos, Marcus, Markel)
French, meaning 'from the god Mars'.

Marcel
(alt. Marcelino, Marcello)
French, meaning 'little warrior'.

Marek
Polish variant of Mark, meaning 'from the god Mars'.

Mariano
Latin, meaning 'from the god Mars'.

Mario
(alt. Marius)
Latin, meaning 'manly'.

Mark
English, meaning 'from the god Mars'.

Marley
(alt. Marlin)
Old English, meaning 'meadow near the lake'.

Marlon
English, meaning 'like little hawk'. Famous as the forename of Marlon Brando.

Marshall
Old French, meaning 'caretaker of horses'.

Martin
Latin, meaning 'dedicated to Mars'.

M

Marty

Shortened form of Martin, meaning 'dedicated to Mars'.

Marvel

English, from the word 'marvel'.

Marvin

Welsh, meaning 'sea friend'.

Mason

English, from the word 'mason'.

Massimo

Italian, meaning 'greatest'.

Mathias
(alt. Matthias)

Hebrew, meaning 'gift of God'.

Mathieu

French form of Matthew, meaning 'gift of God'.

Matthew

Hebrew, meaning 'gift of the Lord'.

Maurice
(alt. Mauricio)

Latin, meaning 'dark skinned' or 'Moorish'.

Maverick

American origin, meaning 'non-conformist leader'.

Max
(alt. Maxie, Maxim)

Latin, meaning 'greatest'.

Maximillian

Latin, meaning 'greatest'.

Maximino

Latin, meaning 'little Max'.

Maxwell

Latin, meaning 'Maccus' stream'.

Maynard

Old German, meaning 'brave'.

McArthur

Scottish, meaning 'son of Arthur'.

McCoy

Scottish, meaning 'son of Coy'.

Mearl

English, meaning 'my earl'.

M

Mederic
French, meaning 'doctor'.

Mekhi
African, meaning 'who is God?'

Mel
Gaelic, meaning 'smooth brow'.

Melbourne
From the city in Australia.

Melchior
Persian, meaning 'king of the city'.

Melton
English, meaning 'town of Mel'.

Melva
Hawaiian, meaning 'plumeria'.

Melville
Scottish, meaning 'town of Mel'.

Melvin
(alt. Melvyn)
English, meaning 'smooth brow'.

Memphis
Greek, meaning 'established and beautiful'. Also the name of a city in the USA.

Mercer
English, from the word 'mercer'.

Merl
French, meaning 'blackbird'.

Merlin
Welsh, meaning 'sea fortress'.

Merrick
Welsh, meaning 'Moorish'.

Merrill
Gaelic, meaning 'shining sea'.

Merritt
English, from the word 'merit'.

Merton
Old English, meaning 'town by the lake'.

Meyer
Hebrew, meaning 'bright farmer'.

Michael

Hebrew, meaning 'resembles God'. One of the archangels.

Michalis

Greek form of Michael, meaning 'resembles God'.

Michel

French form of Michael, meaning 'resembles God'.

Michelangelo

Italian, meaning 'Michael's angel'. Name of the famous painter.

Michele

Italian form of Michael, meaning 'resembles God'.

Michio

Japanese, meaning 'a man with the strength of three thousand men'.

Mickey

Variant of Michael meaning 'resembles God'. Often associated with the Disney character Mickey Mouse.

Miguel

Spanish form of Michael, meaning 'resembles God'.

Mike

Shortened form of Michael, meaning 'resembles God'.

Miklos

Greek form of Michael, meaning 'resembles God'.

Milan

From the name of the Italian city.

Miles

(alt. Milo, Milos, Myles)

English, from the word 'miles'.

Milton

English, meaning 'miller's town'. Also the name of the poet.

Miro

Slavic, meaning 'peace'.

Misha

Russian, meaning 'who is like God'.

Football players

Alan (Shearer)
Ashley (Cole)
Frank (Lampard)
Gary (Lineker)
Gordon (Banks)
Kenny (Dalglish)
Ian (Rush)
Paul (Gascoigne)
Rio (Ferdinand)
Tony (Adams)

Mitch

Shortened form of Mitchell, meaning 'who is like God'.

Mitchell

English, meaning 'who is like God'.

Modesto

Italian, meaning 'modest'.

Moe

Hebrew, meaning 'God's helmet'.

Mohamed

(alt. Mohammad, Mohamet, Mohammed)

Arabic, meaning 'praiseworthy'.

Monroe

Gaelic, meaning 'mouth of the river Rotha'.

Monserrate

Latin, meaning 'jagged mountain'.

Montague

French, meaning 'pointed hill'.

Montana

Latin, meaning 'mountain'. Also a state in the USA.

Monte

Italian, meaning 'mountain'.

Montgomery

Variant of Montague, meaning 'pointed hill'.

Monty

Shortened form of Montague, meaning 'pointed hill'.

Moody

English, from the word 'moody'.

Mordecai

Hebrew, meaning 'little man'.

M

Morgan
Welsh, meaning 'circling sea'.

Moritz
Latin, meaning 'dark skinned and Moorish'.

Morpheus
Greek, meaning 'shape'.

Morris
Welsh, meaning 'dark skinned and Moorish'.

Morrison
English, meaning 'son of Morris'.

Mortimer
French, meaning 'dead sea'.

Morton
Old English, meaning 'moor town'.

Moses
(alt. Moshe, Moshon)
Hebrew, meaning 'saviour'. In the Bible, Moses receives the Ten Commandments from God.

Moss
English, from the word 'moss'.

Muir
Gaelic, meaning 'of the moor'.

Mungo
Gaelic, meaning 'most dear'.

Murl
French, meaning 'blackbird'.

Murphy
Irish, meaning 'sea warrior'.

Murray
Gaelic, meaning 'lord and master'.

Mustafa
Arabic, meaning 'chosen'.

Myron
Greek, meaning 'myrrh'.

Mwita
African, meaning 'humourous one'.

Boys' names

Nairn

Scottish, meaning 'alder-tree river'.

Najee

Arabic, meaning 'dear companion'.

Nakia

Arabic, meaning 'pure'.

Nakul

Indian, meaning 'mongoose'.

Naphtali

Hebrew, meaning 'wrestling'.

Napoleon

Italian origin, meaning 'man from Naples'. Name of the French general who became Emperor of France.

Narciso

Latin, from the myth of Narcissus, famous for drowning after falling in love with his own reflection.

Nash

English, meaning 'at the ash tree'.

Nasir

Arabic, meaning 'helper'.

Nate

Hebrew, meaning 'God has given'.

N

Popular song names

Adam (*Adam's Son*, Blink 182)
Al (*You Can Call Me Al*, Paul Simon)
Anthony (*Movin' Out*, Billy Joel)
Daniel (*Daniel*, Elton John)
Frankie (*Frankie*, Sister Sledge)
Jimmy (*Jimmy Mack*, Martha Reeves and the Vandellas)
Joe (*Hey Joe*, Jimi Hendrix)
Maxwell (*Maxwell's Silver Hammer*, The Beatles)
Robert (*Doctor Robert*, The Beatles)
William (*William It Was Really Nothing*, The Smiths)

Nathan
(alt. Nathaniel)
Hebrew, meaning 'God has given'.

Naval
Indian, meaning 'wonder'.

Naveen
Indian, meaning 'new'.

Neal
Irish, meaning 'champion'.

Ned
Nickname for Edward, meaning 'wealthy guard'.

Neftali
Hebrew, meaning 'struggling'.

Nehemiah
Hebrew, meaning 'comforter'.

Neil
(alt. Niall)
Irish, meaning 'champion'.

Neilson
Irish, meaning 'son of Neil'.

Nelson
Variant of Neil, meaning 'champion'.

Nemo
Latin, meaning 'nobody'.

N

Neo
Latin, meaning 'new'.

Nephi
Greek, meaning 'cloud'.

Nessim
Arabic, meaning 'breeze'.

Nestor
Greek, meaning 'traveller'.

Neville
Old French, meaning 'new village'.

Newland
(alt. Newlands, Newland, Neuland)
English, meaning 'from a new land'.

Newton
English, meaning 'new town'.

Nicholas
(alt. Niklas)
Greek, meaning 'victorious'.

Nick
(alt. Niko, Nikos)
Shortened form of Nicholas, meaning 'victorious'.

Nico
Variant of Nicholas, meaning 'victorious'.

Nigel
Gaelic, meaning 'champion'.

Nikhil
Hindi, meaning 'whole' or 'entire'.

Nikita
Greek, meaning 'unconquered'.

Nikolai
Russian variant of Nicholas, meaning 'victorious'.

Nimrod
Hebrew, meaning 'we will rebel'.

Ninian
Gaelic, associated with the 5th-century saint of the same name.

Nissim
Hebrew, meaning 'wonderful things'.

N

Noah
Hebrew, meaning 'peaceful'.

Noel
French, meaning 'Christmas'.

Nolan
Gaelic, meaning 'champion'.

Norbert
Old German, meaning 'Northern brightness'.

Norman
Old German, meaning 'Northerner'.

Normand
French, meaning 'from Normandy'.

Norris
Old French, meaning 'Northerner'.

Norton
English, meaning 'Northern town'.

Norval
French, meaning 'Northern town'.

Norwood
English, meaning 'Northern forest'.

Nova
Latin, meaning 'new'.

Nuno
Latin, meaning 'ninth'.

Nunzio
Italian, meaning 'messenger'.

Nyoka
African, meaning 'like a snake'.

Names of gods

Apollo (Music: Greek)
Eros (Love: Greek)
Hermes (Messenger of the gods)
Janus (Gates and Doors: Roman)
Mars (War: Roman)
Neptune (Sea: Roman)
Odin (Chief god: Norse)
Ra (Sun: Egyptian)
Thor (Thunder: Norse)

Boys' names

Oakley

English, meaning 'from the oak meadow'.

Obadiah

Biblical, meaning 'God's worker'.

Obama

African, meaning 'crooked'. Made famous by the American President Barack Obama.

Obed

Hebrew, meaning 'servant of God'.

Spelling options

El vs IA (Neil or Niall)
CK vs K (Nick or Nik)
O vs A (Johnathon or Johnathan)
QUE vs CK (Jacques or Jack)

O

Oberon

Old German, meaning 'royal bear'. The Fairy King in *A Midsummer Night's Dream*.

Obijulu

African, meaning 'one who has been consoled'.

Obie

Shortened form of Oberon, meaning 'royal bear'.

Octave

(alt. Octavian, Octavio)

Latin, meaning 'eight'.

Oda

(alt. Odell, Odie, Odis)

Hebrew, meaning 'praise God'.

Ogden

Old English, meaning 'oak valley'.

Oisin

(alt. Ossian)

Celtic, meaning 'fawn'. The name of an ancient Irish poet.

Ola

Norse, meaning 'precious'.

Olaf

(alt. Olan)

Old Norse, meaning 'ancestor'.

Oleander

Hawaiian, meaning 'joyous'.

Oleg

(alt. Olen)

Russian, meaning 'holy'.

Olin

Russian, meaning 'rock'.

Oliver

Latin, meaning 'olive tree'.

Olivier

French form of Oliver, meaning 'olive tree'.

Ollie

Shortened form of Oliver, meaning 'olive tree'.

Omar

(alt. Omari, Omarion)

Arabic, meaning 'speaker'.

Ondrej

Czech, meaning 'manly'.

O

Ora
Latin, meaning 'hour'.

Oran
(alt. Oren, Orrin)
Gaelic, meaning 'light and pale'.

Orange
English, from the word 'orange'.

Orion
From the Greek hunter.

Orlando
(alt. Orlo)
Old German, meaning 'old land'. Name of a city in the USA.

Orpheus
Greek, meaning 'beautiful voice'.

Orrick
English, meaning 'sword ruler'.

Orson
Latin, meaning 'bear'.

Orville
Old French, meaning 'gold town'.

Osaka
From the Japanese city.

Osborne
Norse, meaning 'bear god'.

Oscar
Old English, meaning 'spear of the Gods'.

Osias
Hebrew, meaning 'salvation'.

Foreign alternatives

David – Dafydd, Davin
John – Jean, Giovanni, Juan
Michael – Miguel, Mikhail
Peter – Pedro, Pierre, Pyotr, Piers
Rory – Ruaridh

O

Oswald
German, meaning 'God's power'.

Otha
(alt. Otho)
German, meaning 'wealth'.

Othello
From the Shakespearean character.

Otis
German, meaning 'wealth'.

Otten
English, meaning 'otter-like'.

Otto
Italian, meaning 'eight'.

Ovid
Latin, meaning 'sheep'. Associated with the Roman poet.

Owain
Welsh, meaning 'youth'.

Owen
Welsh, meaning 'well born and noble'.

Oz
Hebrew, meaning 'strength'.

Popular Asian names for boys and girls

Aoi
Chang
Fang
Hiro
Hiroshi
Iku
Murasaki
Niu
Rei
Zinan

P

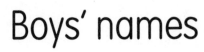

Boys' names

Pablo
Spanish, meaning 'little'.

Paco
Native American, meaning 'eagle'. Also a Spanish alternative for Francisco.

Padma
Indian, meaning 'lotus'.

Padraig
Irish, meaning 'noble'.

Panos
Greek, meaning 'all holy'.

Paolo
Italian, meaning 'little'.

Paresh
Indian, meaning 'supreme standard'.

Paris
From France's capital city. Also the trojan prince in Homer's *Iliad* and Juliet's suitor in Shakespeare's *Romeo and Juliet*.

Pascal
Latin, meaning 'Easter child'.

Pat
Shortened form of Patrick, meaning 'noble'.

Patrice
Variant of Patrick, meaning 'noble'.

P

Patrick
Irish, meaning 'noble'.

Patten
English, meaning 'noble'.

Paul
Biblical, meaning 'small'.

Pavel
Latin, meaning 'small'.

Pax
Latin, meaning 'peace'.

Paxton
English, meaning 'town of peace'.

Payne
Latin, meaning 'peasant'.

Payton
Latin, meaning 'peasant's town'.

Pedro
Spanish form of Peter, meaning 'rock'.

Penn
English, meaning 'hill'.

Percival
French, meaning 'pierce the valley'.

Percy
Shortened form of Percival, meaning 'pierce the valley'.

Perez
Hebrew, meaning 'breach'.

Pericles
Greek, meaning 'far-famed'.

Perrin
Greek, meaning 'rock'.

Perry
English, meaning 'rock'.

Pervis
English, meaning 'purveyor'.

Pesah
(alt. Pesach, Pesasch)
Hebrew, meaning 'spared'.

Pete
Shortened form of Peter, meaning 'rock'.

P

Peter
English, meaning 'rock'.

Petros
Spanish form of Peter, meaning 'rock'.

Peyton
Old English, meaning 'fighting man's estate'.

Phil
Shortened form of Philip, meaning 'lover of horses'.

Phileman
Greek, meaning 'affectionate'.

Philip
Greek, meaning 'lover of horses'.

Philo
Greek, meaning 'love'.

Phineas
(alt. Pinchas)
Hebrew, meaning 'oracle'.

Phoenix
Greek, meaning 'dark red'.

Pierre
French form of Peter, meaning 'stone'.

Piers
Greek form of Peter, meaning 'rock'.

Pierson
Variant of Peirce, meaning 'son of Piers'.

Pip
Greek, shortened form of Philip, meaning 'lover of horses'.

Placido
Latin, meaning 'placid'.

No-nickname names

Alex
Jude
Keith
Otto
Owen
Toby

P

Porthos

From the character in *The Three Musketeers* by Alexandre Dumas.

Pradeep

Hindi, meaning 'light'.

Pranav

Hindi, meaning 'spiritual leader'.

Presley

Old English, meaning 'priest's meadow'.

Preston

Old English, meaning 'priest's town'.

Primo

Italian, meaning 'first'.

Primus

Latin, meaning 'first'.

Prince

English, from the word 'prince'.

Proctor

(alt. Prockter, Procter)

Latin, meaning 'steward'.

> ## Popular Australian names for boys and girls
>
> Ava
> Cooper
> Ella
> Ethan
> Griffiths
> Lachlan
> Mia
> Riley
> Sienna
> Tallara

Prospero

Latin, meaning 'prosperous'.

Pryor

English, meaning 'first'.

Ptolemy

Greek, meaning 'aggressive' or 'warlike'.

Purvis

(alt. Purves, Purviss)

French, meaning 'purveyor'.

Boys' names

Qino
Chinese, meaning 'handsome'.

Quabil
Arabic, meaning 'able'.

Quadim
Arabic, meaning 'able'.

Quadir
Arabic, meaning 'powerful'.

Quaid
Irish, meaning 'fourth'.

Qued
Native American, meaning 'weaver of a decorated robe'.

Quemby
Norse, meaning 'from the woman's estate'.

Quentin
(alt. Quinten, Quintin, Quinton, Quintus)
Latin, meaning 'fifth'.

Quillan
Gaelic, meaning 'sword'.

Quillon
Gaelic, meaning 'club'.

Quincy
Old French, meaning 'estate of the fifth son'.

Q

Quinlan
Gaelic, meaning 'fit, shapely and strong'.

Quinn
Gaelic, meaning 'counsel'.

Quinton
English, meaning 'queen's community'.

'Powerful' names

Bernon
Derek
Hercules
Logan
Oswald
Sampson
Thor
Titus
Warren
Zane

R
Boys' names

Radames
Slavic, meaning 'famous joy'.

Raekwon
Hebrew, meaning 'God has healed'.

Rafael
(alt. Rafe, Rafer, Raffi, Raphael)
Hebrew, meaning 'God has healed'. One of the archangels.

Ragnar
Old Norse, meaning 'judgement warrior'.

Raheem
Arabic, meaning 'merciful and kind'.

Rahm
Hebrew, meaning 'pleasing'.

Rahul
(alt. Raoul, Raul)
Indian, meaning 'efficient'.

Raiden
(alt. Rainen)
From the Japanese god of thunder.

Rainer
Alternative of Raynor, meaning 'deciding warrior'.

Raj
Indian, meaning 'king'.

Rajesh
(alt. Ramesh)
Indian, meaning 'ruler of kings'.

R

Raleigh

Old English, meaning 'deer's meadow'.

Ralph

Old English, meaning 'wolf'.

Ram

English, from the word 'ram'.

Ramiro

Germanic, meaning 'powerful in battle'.

Ramone

Spanish, meaning 'wise supporter' or 'romantic'.

Ramsey
(alt. Ramsay)

Old English, meaning 'wild garlic island'.

Randall
(alt. Randolph)

Old German, meaning 'wolf shield'.

Randy

Variant of Randall, meaning 'wolf shield'. In modern English, randy can also mean amorous.

Raniel

English, meaning 'God is my happiness'.

Ranjit

Indian, meaning 'influenced by charm'.

Rannoch

Gaelic, meaning 'fern'.

Rashad

Arabic, meaning 'good judgment'.

Rasheed
(alt. Rashid)

Indian, meaning 'rightly guided'.

Rasmus

Greek, meaning 'beloved'.

Raven

English, from the word 'raven'.

Ravi

French, meaning 'delighted'.

Rawlins

French alternative of Roland, meaning 'renowned land'.

R

Ray

English, from the word 'ray'.

Raymond

(alt. Rayner)

English, meaning 'advisor'.

Raz

Israeli, meaning 'secret' or 'mystery'.

Reagan

Irish, meaning 'little king'.

Reggie

Latin, meaning 'regal'.

Reginald

Latin, meaning 'regal'.

Regis

Shortened form of Reginald, meaning 'regal'.

Reid

Old English, meaning 'by the reeds'.

Reilly

English, meaning 'courageous'.

Remington

English, meaning 'ridge town'.

Remus

Latin, meaning 'swift'.

Rémy

French, meaning 'from Rheims'.

Ren

Shortened form of Reginald, meaning 'regal'.

Renato

Latin, meaning 'rebirth'.

Rene

French, meaning 'rebirth'.

Reno

Latin, meaning 'renewed'.

Reuben

Spanish, meaning 'a son'.

Reuel

Hebrew, meaning 'friend of God'.

R

Rex

Latin, meaning 'king'.

Rey

Spanish, meaning 'king'.

Reynold

Latin, meaning 'king's advisor'.

Rhodes

German, meaning 'where the roses grow'. Also the name of the Greek town.

Rhodri

Welsh, meaning 'ruler of the circle'.

Rhys

Welsh, meaning 'enthusiasm'.

Ricardo

Spanish alternative of Richard, meaning 'powerful leader'.

Richard

Old German, meaning 'powerful leader'.

Richie

Shortened form of Richard, meaning 'powerful leader'.

Rick

Shortened form of Richard, meaning 'powerful leader'.

Ricki

Shortened form of Richard, meaning 'powerful leader'.

Ricky

Shortened form of Richard, meaning 'powerful leader'.

Ridley

English, meaning 'cleared wood'.

Rigby

English, meaning 'valley of the ruler'.

Ringo

English, meaning 'ring'.

Rio

Spanish, meaning 'river'.

Riordan

Gaelic, meaning 'bard'.

R

Rishi

Variant of Richard, meaning 'powerful leader'.

Ritchie

Shortened form of Richard, meaning 'powerful leader'.

Roald

Scandinavian, meaning 'ruler'.

Rob

Shortened form of Robert, meaning 'bright fame'.

Robbie

Shortened form of Robert, meaning 'bright fame'.

Robert

Old German, meaning 'bright fame'.

Roberto

Variant of Robert, meaning 'bright fame'.

Robin

English, from the word 'robin'.

Robinson

English, meaning 'son of Robin'.

Rocco

(alt. Rocky)

Italian, meaning 'rest'.

Rockwell

English, meaning 'of the rock well'.

Rod

Short for Rhodri, Roderick and Rodney.

Roderick

German, meaning 'famous power'.

Rodney

Old German, meaning 'island near the clearing'.

Rodrigo

Spanish form of Roderick, meaning 'famous power'.

Roger

Old German, meaning 'spear man'.

Roland

Old German, meaning 'renowned land'.

R

Rolf

Old German, meaning 'wolf'.

Rollie
(alt. Rollo)

Old German, meaning 'renowned land'.

Roman

Latin, meaning 'from Rome'.

Romeo

Latin, meaning 'pilgrim to Rome'. Made famous by Shakespeare's play.

Romulus

Latin, meaning 'Roman'. Romulus and his twin brother Remus were the founders of Rome.

Ron
(alt. Ronnie)

Shortened form of Ronald, meaning 'mountain of strength'.

Ronald

Norse, meaning 'mountain of strength'.

Ronan

Gaelic, meaning 'little seal'.

Rory

English, meaning 'red king'.

Ross
(alt. Russ)

Scottish, meaning 'cape'.

Rowan
(alt. Roan)

Gaelic, meaning 'little red one'. Also reference to the rowan tree.

Roy

Gaelic, meaning 'red'.

Ruben

Hebrew, meaning 'son'.

Rudolph

Old German, meaning 'famous wolf'.

Rudy

Shortened form of Rudolph, meaning 'famous wolf'.

Rufus

Latin, meaning 'red-haired'.

Rupert

Variant of Robert, meaning 'bright fame'.

Russell

Old French, meaning 'little red one'.

Ruslan

Russian, meaning 'like a lion'.

Rusty

English, meaning 'ruddy'.

Ryan

Gaelic, meaning 'little king'.

Ryder

English, meaning 'horseman'.

Rye

English, from the word 'rye'.

Ryker

From Richard, meaning 'powerful leader'.

Rylan

English, meaning 'land where rye is grown'.

Ryley

Old English, meaning 'rye clearing'.

Ryu

Japanese, meaning 'dragon'.

S

Boys' names

Saar
Hebrew, meaning 'tempest'.

Saber
French, meaning 'sword'.

Sagar
African, meaning 'ruler of the water'.

Sage
English, meaning 'wise'.

Sakari
Native American, meaning 'sweet'.

Salil
Indian, meaning 'from the water'.

Salim
Arabic, meaning 'secure'.

Salvador
Spanish, meaning 'saviour'.

Salvatore
Italian, meaning 'saviour'.

Nautical names

Caspian
Dylan
Merlin
Murphy
Neptune

S

Sam
(alt. Sama, Sammie, Sammy)
Hebrew, meaning 'God is heard'.

Samir
Arabic, meaning 'pleasant companion'.

Samson
Hebrew, meaning 'son of Sam'.

Samuel
Hebrew, meaning 'God is heard'.

Sandeep
Indian, meaning 'lighting the way'.

Sandro
Shortened form of Alessandro, meaning 'defending men'.

Sandy
Shortened form of Alexander, meaning 'defending men'.

Sanjay
Indian, meaning 'victory'.

Santiago
Spanish, meaning 'Saint James'.

Santino
Spanish, meaning 'little Saint James'.

Santo
(alt. Santos)
Latin, meaning 'saint'.

Sascha
Shortened Russian form of Alexander, meaning 'defending men'.

Scott
(alt. Scottie)
English, meaning 'from Scotland'.

Seamus
Irish variant of James, meaning 'he who supplants'.

Sean
(alt. Shaun)
Variant of John, meaning 'God is gracious'.

Sebastian
Greek, meaning 'revered'.

S

Sébastien

French form of Sebastian, meaning 'revered'.

Sergio

Latin, meaning 'servant'.

Seth

Hebrew, meaning 'appointed'.

Severus

Latin, meaning 'severe'. Found as the name of Severus Snape in the *Harry Potter* series.

Seymour

From Saint-Maur in northern France.

Shane

Variant of Sean, meaning 'God is gracious'.

Shalen

Arabic, meaning 'tribal leader'.

Sharif

Arabic, meaning 'honoured'.

Shea

Gaelic, meaning 'admirable'.

Shelby

Norse, meaning 'willow'.

Sherlock

English, meaning 'fair haired'.

Sherman

Old English, meaning 'shear man'.

Shmuel

Hebrew, meaning 'his name is God'.

Shola

Arabic, meaning 'energetic'.

Sid

Shortened form of Sidney, meaning 'wide meadow'.

Names of painters

Claude (Monet)
Francis (Bacon)
Leonardo (da Vinci)
Salvador (Dali)
Vincent (Van Gogh)

S

Sidney
English, meaning 'wide meadow'.

Sigmund
Old German, meaning 'victorious hand'.

Silvanus
(alt. Silvio)
Latin, meaning 'woods'.

Sim
Shortened form of Simba, meaning 'lion'.

Simba
Arabic, meaning 'lion'.

Simon
(alt. Simeon)
Hebrew, meaning 'to hear'.

Sinbad
Literary merchant adventurer.

Sindri
Norse, meaning 'dwarf'.

Sipho
African, meaning 'the unknown one'.

Sire
English, from the word 'sire'.

Sirius
Hebrew, meaning 'brightest star'. Name of Harry Potter's godfather, Sirius Black.

Skipper
English, meaning 'ship captain'.

Skyler
English, meaning 'scholar'.

Socrates
Greek philosopher.

Solomon
Hebrew, meaning 'peace'.

Sonny
American English, meaning 'son'.

Soren
Scandinavian variant of Severus, meaning 'brightest star'.

Spencer
English, meaning 'dispenser'.

S

Spike

English, from the word 'spike'.

Stamos

Greek, meaning 'reasonable'.

Stan

Shortened form of Stanley, meaning 'stony meadow'.

Stanford

English, meaning 'stone ford'.

Stanley

English, meaning 'stony meadow'.

Stavros

Greek, meaning 'crowned'.

Stellan

Latin, meaning 'starred'.

Steno

German, meaning 'stone'.

Stephen

(alt. Stefan, Stefano, Steffan)

English, meaning 'crowned'.

Steven

(alt. Steve, Stevie)

English, meaning 'crowned'.

Stewart

English, meaning 'steward'.

Stoney

English, meaning 'stone like'.

Storm

English, from the word 'storm'.

Stuart

English, meaning 'steward'.

Sven

Norse, meaning 'boy'.

Sydney

English, meaning 'wide meadow'.

Peaceful names

Glade
Manfred
Paxton
Vale
Wilfred

179

S

Syed
Arabic, meaning 'lucky'.

Sylvester
Latin, meaning 'wooded'.

Syon
Indian, meaning 'followed by good'.

T

Boys' names

Tacitus
From the Roman historian.

Tad
English, from the word 'tadpole'.

Taine
Gaelic, meaning 'river'.

Taj
Indian, meaning 'crown'.

Takashi
Japanese, meaning 'praiseworthy'.

Takoda
Sioux, meaning 'friend to everyone'.

Talbot
(alt. Tal)

Aristocratic English name.

Tamir
Arabic, meaning 'tall and wealthy'.

Taras
(alt. Tarez)

Scottish, meaning 'crag'.

Tarek
Arabic, meaning 'evening caller'.

Tarian
Welsh, meaning 'silver'.

T

Tariq
Arabic, meaning 'morning star'.

Tarquin
From the Roman clan name.

Tarun
Hindi, meaning 'young'.

Tatanka
Hebrew, meaning 'bull'.

Tate
English, meaning 'cheerful'.

Taurean
English, meaning 'bull like'.

Tavares
English, meaning 'descendant of the hermit'.

Tave
(alt. Tavian, Tavis, Tavish)
From Octave, meaning 'eight'.

Tavor
Hebrew, meaning 'misfortunate'.

Taylor
English, meaning 'tailor'.

Ted
(alt. Teddy)
English, from Edward, meaning 'wealthy'.

Terence
(alt. Terrill, Terry)
English, meaning 'tender'.

Tex
English, meaning 'Texan'.

Thabo
African, meaning 'filled with happiness'.

Thane
(alt. Thayer)
Scottish, meaning 'landholder'.

Thelonius
Latin, meaning 'ruler of the people'.

Theo
Shortened form of Theodore, meaning 'God's gift'.

Theodore
Greek, meaning 'God's gift'.

T

Theophile
Latin, meaning 'God's love'.

Theron
Greek, meaning 'hunter'.

Thierry
French variant of Terence, meaning 'tender'.

Thomas
Hebrew, meaning 'twin'.

Thomsen
English, meaning 'son of Thomas'.

Thor
Norse, meaning 'thunder'.

Tiago
From Santiago, meaning 'Saint Hebrew, meaning 'nature lover'.

Tibor
Latin, from the river Tiber.

Tien
Vietnamese, meaning 'first'.

Tieman
Gaelic, meaning 'lord'.

Tim
Shortened form of Timothy, meaning 'God's honour'.

Timothy
Greek, meaning 'God's honour'.

Tito
(alt. Titus)
Latin, meaning 'defender'.

Tobias
(alt. Toby)
Hebrew, meaning 'God is good'.

Tod
(alt. Todd)
English, meaning 'fox'.

Tom
(alt. Tomlin, Tommy)
Hebrew, meaning 'twin'.

Tonneau
French, meaning 'barrel'.

Tony
Shortened form of Anthony, from the old Roman family name.

T

Torey
Norse, meaning 'Thor'.

Torin
Gaelic, meaning 'chief'.

Torquil
Gaelic, meaning 'helmet'.

Toshi
Japanese, meaning 'reflection'.

Travis
French, meaning 'crossover'.

Trevor
Welsh origin, meaning 'great settlement'.

Trey
(alt. Tyree)
French, meaning 'very'.

Trevelian
Welsh, meaning 'of the house of Eden'.

Tristan
(alt. Tristram)
From the Celtic hero.

Troy
Gaelic, meaning 'descended from the soldier'.

Tudor
Variant of Theodore, 'God's gift'.

Tyler
English, meaning 'tile maker'.

Tyrell
French, meaning 'puller'.

Tyrone
Gaelic, meaning 'Owen's county'.

Tyson
English, meaning 'son of Tyrone'.

Famous rugby players

Brian (O'Driscoll)
Gavin (Henson)
Jonny (Wilkinson)
Lawrence (Dallaglio)
Martin (Johnson)

Boys' names

Uberto
(alt. Umberto)
From the Italian royal name.

Udath
(alt. Udathel)
Indian, meaning 'noble'.

Udo
German, meaning 'power of the wolf'.

Ugo
Italian form of Hugo, meaning 'mind and heart'.

Ulf
German, meaning 'wolf'.

Ulrich
German, meaning 'noble ruler'.

Ultan
Irish, meaning 'from Ulster'.

Ulysses
Greek, meaning 'wrathful'. Made famous by the mythological voyager.

Unwyn
(alt. Unwin, Unwine)
English, meaning 'unfriendly'.

Upton
English, meaning 'high town'.

Urho
Finnish, meaning 'brave'.

Uri
(alt. Uriah, Urias)
Hebrew, meaning 'my light'.

Uriel

Hebrew, meaning 'angel of light'. One of the archangels.

Usher

English, from the word 'usher'. Made famous by American R&B star.

Uttam

Indian, meaning 'best'.

Uzi

Hebrew, meaning 'my strength'.

Uzzi

(alt. Uzziah)

Hebrew, meaning 'my power'.

Christmas names

Christian
Ebenezer
Gabriel
Joseph
Nicholas
Noel
Wenceslas

V

Boys' names

Vaclav
Czech, meaning 'receives glory'.

Vadim
Russian, meaning 'scandal maker'.

Valdemar
German, meaning 'renowned leader'.

Valente
Latin, meaning 'valiant'.

Valentin
(alt. Val)
French, meaning 'valentine'.

Valentine
English, from the word 'valentine'.

Valentino
Italian, meaning 'valentine'.

Valerio
Italian, meaning 'valiant'.

Valia
Indian, meaning 'king of the monkeys'.

Van
Dutch, meaning 'son of'.

Vance
English, meaning 'marshland'.

V

Vangelis
Greek, meaning 'good news'.

Varun
Hindi, meaning 'water god'.

Vasilis
Greek, meaning 'kingly'.

Vaughan
Welsh, meaning 'little'.

Vernell
French, meaning 'green and flourishing'.

Verner
German, meaning 'army defender'.

Vernon
(alt. Vernie)
French, meaning 'alder grove'.

Versilius
Latin, meaning 'flier'.

Vester
Latin, meaning 'wooded'.

Vibol
Cambodian, meaning 'man of plenty'.

Victor
Latin, meaning 'champion'.

Vidal
(alt. Vidar)
Spanish, meaning 'life giving'.

Vijay
Hindi, meaning 'conquering'.

Vikram
Hindi, meaning 'sun'.

Viktor
Latin, meaning 'victory'.

Ville
French, meaning 'town'.

Vincent
(alt. Vince)
English, meaning 'victorious'.

Virgil
From the Latin poet.

Vito
Spanish, meaning 'life'.

Vittorio

Italian, meaning 'victory'.

Vitus

Latin, meaning 'life'.

Vivek

Indian, meaning 'wisdom'.

Vivian

Latin, meaning 'lively'.

Vladimir

Slavic, meaning 'prince'.

Volker

German, meaning 'defender of the people'.

Von

Norse, meaning 'hope'.

V

W

Boys' names

Wade

English, meaning 'to move forward' or 'to go'.

Waldemar

German, meaning 'famous ruler'.

Walden

English, meaning 'valley of the Britons'.

Waldo

Old German, meaning 'rule'.

Walker

English, meaning 'a fuller'.

Wallace

English, meaning 'foreigner' or 'stranger'.

Wally

German, meaning 'ruler of the army'.

Walter

(alt. Walt)

German, meaning 'ruler of the army'.

Wasim

Arabic, meaning 'attractive' or 'full of grace'.

Ward

English, meaning 'guardian'.

Wardell

Old English, meaning 'watchman's hill'.

Warner

German, meaning 'army guard'.

Warren

German, meaning 'guard' or 'the game park'.

Warwick

English, meaning 'farm near the weir'.

Washington

English, meaning 'clever' or 'clever man's settlement'.

Wassily

Greek, meaning 'royal' or 'kingly'.

Watson

English, meaning 'son' or 'son of Walter'.

Waverley
(alt. Waverly)

English, meaning 'quaking aspen'.

Waylon

English, meaning 'land by the road'.

Wayne

English, meaning 'a cartwright'.

Webster

English, meaning 'weaver'.

Weldon

English, meaning 'from the hill of well' or 'hill with a well'.

Wendell
(alt. Wendel)

German, meaning 'a wend'.

Werner

German, meaning 'army guard'.

Werther

German, meaning 'a soldier in the army'.

Weston

English, meaning 'from the west town'.

Wheeler

English, meaning 'wheel maker'.

Whitley

English, meaning 'white wood'.

Whitman

Old English, meaning 'white man'.

Whitney

Old English, meaning 'white island'.

Wilber
(alt. Wilbur)

Old German, meaning 'bright will'.

Wildon

English, meaning 'wooded hill'.

Wiley

Old English, meaning 'beguiling' or 'enchanting'.

Wilford

Old English, meaning 'the ford by the willows'.

Wilfredo
(alt. Wilfred, Wilfrid)

English, meaning 'to will peace'.

Wilhelm

German, meaning 'strong-willed warrior'.

Wilkes
(alt. Wilkie)

Old English, meaning 'strong-willed protector' or 'strong and resolute protector'.

William
(alt. Will, Willie)

English (Teutonic), meaning 'strong protector' or 'strong-willed warrior'.

Willis

English, meaning 'server of Will'.

Willoughby

Old Norse and Old English, meaning 'from the farm by the trees'.

Wilmer

English (Teutonic), meaning 'famously resolute'.

Wilmot

English, meaning 'resolute mind'.

Wilson

English, meaning 'son of William'.

Wilton

Old Norse and English, meaning 'from the farm by the brook' or 'from the farm by the streams'.

Windell
(alt. Wendell)

German, meaning 'wanderer' or 'seeker'.

Knights of the round table

Arthur
Gareth
Gawain
Lancelot
Tristram

Windsor

Old English, meaning 'river bank' or 'landing place'.

Winton

Old English, meaning 'a friend's farm'.

Winfield

English, meaning 'from the field of Wina'.

Wirrin

Aboriginal, meaning 'a tea tree'.

Winslow

Old English, meaning 'victory on the hill'.

Wistan

Old English, meaning 'battle stone' or 'mark of the battle'.

Winter

Old English, meaning 'to be born in the winter'.

Wittan

Old English, meaning 'farm in the woods' or 'farm by the woods'.

Winthrop

Old English, meaning 'village of friends'.

Wolf
(alt. Wolfe)

English, meaning 'strong as a wolf'.

Wolfgang

Teutonic, meaning 'the path of wolves'.

Wolfrom

Teutonic, meaning 'raven wolf'.

Wolter

Dutch, a form of Walter meaning 'ruler of the army'.

Woodburn

Old English, meaning 'a stream in the woods'.

Woodrow

English, meaning 'from the row of houses by the wood'.

Woodward

English, meaning 'guardian of the forest'.

Woody

American, meaning 'path in the woods'.

Worcester

Old English, meaning 'from a Roman site'.

Worth

American, meaning 'worth much' or 'wealthy place' or 'wealth and riches'.

Wren

Old English, meaning 'tiny bird'.

Wright

Old English, meaning 'to be a craftsman' or 'from a carpenter'.

Wyatt

Teutonic, meaning 'from wood' or 'from the wide water'.

Wyclef

(alt. Wycleff, Wycliff, Wycliffe)

English, meaning 'inhabitant of the white cliff'.

Wynn

(alt. Wyn)

Welsh, meaning 'very blessed' or 'the fair blessed one'.

W

Popular English names for boys and girls

Alec
Alice
Blake
Chelsea
Edward
Gavin
Hazel
Marilyn
Oscar
Primrose

Boys' names

Xadrian

American, a combination of X and Adrian, meaning 'from Hadria'.

Xander

Greek, meaning 'defender of the people'.

Xannon

American, meaning 'descendent of an ancient family'.

Xanthus

Greek, meaning 'golden-haired'.

Xavier

Latin, meaning 'to the new house'.

Xenon

Greek, meaning 'the guest'.

Xerxes

Persian, meaning 'ruler of the people' or 'respected king'.

Xeven

Slavic, meaning 'lively'.

Xylander

Greek, meaning 'man of the forest'.

Bird names

Gannet
Phoenix
Robin
Tern
Wren

Boys' names

Yaal

Hebrew, meaning 'ascending' or 'one to ascend'.

Yadid

Hebrew, meaning 'the beloved one'.

Yadon

Hebrew, meaning 'against judgment'.

Yahir

Spanish, meaning 'handsome one'.

Yaholo

Native American, meaning 'yells'.

Yakiya

Hebrew, meaning 'pure' or 'bright'.

Yair

Hebrew, meaning 'the enlightening one' or 'illuminating'.

Yanis
(alt. Yannis)

Greek, a form of John meaning 'gift of God'.

Yarden

Hebrew, meaning 'to flow downward'.

Ye

Chinese, meaning 'bright one' or 'light'.

Y

Yehuda

Hebrew, meaning 'to praise and exalt'.

Yered

Hebrew, a form of Jared, meaning 'descending'.

Yerik

Russian, meaning 'God-appointed one'.

Yerodin

African, meaning 'studious'.

Yervant

Armenian, meaning 'King of people'.

Yitzak
(alt. Yitzaak)

Hebrew, meaning 'laughter' or 'one who laughs'.

Ynyr

Welsh, meaning 'to honour'.

Yobachi

African, meaning 'one who prays to God' or 'prayed to God'.

Yogi

Japanese, meaning 'one who practises yoga' or 'from yoga'.

Yoloti

Aztec, meaning 'heart'.

Yona

Native American, meaning 'bear'; Hebrew, meaning 'dove'.

York

Celtic, meaning 'yew tree' or 'from the farm of the yew tree'.

Yosef

Hebrew, meaning 'added by God' or 'God shall add'.

Yuri

Aboriginal, meaning 'to hear'; Japanese, meaning 'one to listen'; Russian, a form of George meaning 'farmer'.

Yuuta

Japanese, meaning 'excellent'.

Yves

French, meaning 'miniature archer' or 'small archer'.

Z Boys' names

Zachariah
(alt. Zac, Zach, Zachary)
Hebrew, meaning 'remembered by the Lord' or 'God has remembered'.

Zad
Persian, meaning 'my son'.

Zada
(alt. Zadan, Zadin, Zadun)
Dutch, meaning 'a man who sowed seeds'.

Zadok
Hebrew, meaning 'righteous one'.

Zador
Hungarian, meaning 'violent demeanour'.

Zafar
Arabic, meaning 'triumphant'.

Zaid
African, meaning 'increase the growth' or 'growth'.

Zaide
Yiddish, meaning 'the elder ones'.

Zain
(alt. Zane)
Arabic, meaning 'the handsome son'.

Zaire
African, meaning 'river from Zaire'.

Z

Zander

Greek, meaning 'defender of my people'.

Zarek

Persian, meaning 'God protect our King'.

Zoltan

(alt. Zoltin)

Hungarian, meaning 'life'.

Fiery names

Aidan
Blaze
Flint
Kenneth

part three

Girls' Names

A Girls' names

A'mari

Variation on the Swahili or Muslim name Amira, meaning 'princess'.

Aanya

Variation on the Russian name Anya, meaning 'favour' or 'grace'. Also of Sanskrit origin, meaning 'the inexhaustible'.

Aaryanna

Derivative of the Latin name Ariadne and the Greek Ariadne, both meaning 'the very holy one'.

Abby
(alt. Abbey, Abbie)

Form of Abigail, meaning 'my father's joy' in Hebrew.

Abigail
(alt. Abagail, Abbiegayle, Abbigail, Abigale, Abigayle)

Hebrew, meaning 'my father's joy'.

Abilene
(alt. Abilee)

Latin and Spanish for 'hazelnut'.

Abra

Female variation of Abraham. Also of Sanskrit origin, meaning 'clouds'.

Abina
(alt. Abena)

Ghanaian, meaning 'born on Tuesday'.

Abril

Spanish for the month of April. Also of Latin origin, meaning 'open'.

Acacia

Greek, meaning 'point' or 'thorn'. Also a species of flowering trees and shrubs.

Acadia

A variation of the Greek word arcadia meaning 'paradise'. Originally, a French colony in Canada.

Ada
(alt. Adair)

Hebrew, meaning 'adornment'.

Adalee

German, meaning 'noble'.

Adalia

Hebrew, meaning 'God is my refuge'.

Addie
(alt. Addy, Adi)

Abbreviated form of Addison, Adelaide, Adele and Adeline.

Addison
(alt. Addisyn, Addyson)

English, meaning 'son of Adam'.

Adelaide
(alt. Adelaida)

German, popular after the rule of William IV and Queen Adelaide of England in the 19th century.

Adele
(alt. Adela, Adelia, Adell, Adella, Adelle)

German, meaning 'noble' or 'nobility'.

Adeline
(alt. Adalyn, Adalynn, Adelina, Adelyn)

Variant of Adelaide, meaning 'nobility'.

Aden
(alt. Addien)

Hebrew, meaning 'decoration'.

Aderyn

Welsh, meaning 'bird'.

Adesina

Nigerian, meaning 'she paves the way'. Usually given to a first-born daughter.

A

Adeola
(alt. Adeolah, Adeolla)

African, meaning 'weaver of a crown of honour'.

Adia

Variant of Ada, meaning 'adornment'.

Adina
(alt. Adena)

Hebrew, meaning 'high hopes' or 'precious'.

Adira

Hebrew, meaning 'noble' or 'powerful'.

Adrian

Italian, from the northern city of Adria.

Adrianna
(alt. Adriana)

Variant of Adrienne, meaning 'rich' or 'dark'.

Adrienne
(alt. Adriane, Adrianne)

Greek, meaning 'rich', or Latin, meaning 'dark'.

Aegle

Greek, meaning 'brightness' or 'splendour'.

Movie inspirations

Bridget (*Bridget Jones's Diary*)
Cady (*Mean Girls*)
Fiona (*Shrek*)
Holly (*Breakfast at Tiffany's*)
Lara (*Tomb Raider*)
Maria (*The Sound of Music*)
Marla (*Fight Club*)
Mary (*Mary Poppins*)
Pandora (*Avatar*)
Trinity (*The Matrix*)

A

Aerin

Variant of Erin, meaning 'peace-making'.

Aerith

American, from a character in the computer game *Final Fantasy VII*.

Aero
(alt. Aeron)

Greek, meaning 'water'.

Aerolynn

Combination of the Greek Aero, meaning 'water', and the English Lynn, meaning 'waterfall'.

Afia
(alt. Aff, Affi)

Arabic, meaning 'a child born on Friday'.

Africa

Celtic for 'pleasant', as well as the name of the continent.

Afsaneh

Iranian, meaning 'a fairy tale'.

Afsha

Persian, meaning 'one who sprinkles light'.

Afton

Originally a place name in Scotland.

Agatha

From Saint Agatha, the patron saint of bells, meaning 'good'.

Aglaia

One of the three Greek Graces, meaning 'brilliance'.

Agnes

Greek, meaning 'virginal' or 'pure'.

Agrippina

From the Latin expression, meaning 'born feet first'.

Aida

Arabic, meaning 'reward' or 'present'.

Aidanne
(alt. Aidan, Aidenn)

Gaelic, meaning 'fire'.

Ailbhe

Irish, meaning 'noble' or 'bright'.

A

Aileen
(alt. Aelinn, Aleen, Aline, Alline, Eileen)
A Gaelic variant of Helen, meaning 'light'.

Ailith
(alt. Ailish)
Old English, meaning 'seasoned warrior'.

Ailsa
Scottish, meaning 'pledge from God', as well as the name of a Scottish island, Ailsa Craig.

Aimee
(alt. Aimie, Amie)
The French spelling of Amy, meaning 'beloved'.

Aina
Scandinavian, meaning 'forever'.

Aine
(alt. Aino)
Celtic, meaning 'happiness'.

Ainsley
Scottish and Gaelic, meaning 'one's own meadow'.

Aisha
(alt. Aeysha)
Arabic, meaning 'woman'; as well as Swahili, meaning 'life'.

Aishwarya
Variant on the Arabic Aisha, meaning 'woman'.

Aislinn
(alt. Aislin, Aisling, Aislyn, Alene, Allene)
Irish Gaelic, meaning 'dream'.

Aiyanna
(alt. Aiyana)
Native American, meaning 'forever flowering'.

Aja
Hindi, meaning 'goat'.

Aka
(alt. Akah, Akkah)
Maori, meaning 'loving one'.

Akela
(alt. Akilah)
Hawaiian, meaning 'noble'.

Akilina
Greek or Russian, meaning 'eagle'.

Akiva

Hebrew, meaning 'protect and shelter'.

Alaina

(alt. Alane, Alani, Alayna, Aleena)

Feminine of Alan, originating from the French for 'rock' or 'comely'.

Alana

(alt. Alanna, Alannah)

Variant of Alaina, meaning 'rock' or 'comely'.

Alanis

(alt. Alarice)

Variant of Alaina, meaning 'rock' or 'comely'.

Alba

Latin, meaning 'white'. Also the Gaelic word for 'Scotland'.

Alberta

(alt. Albertha, Albertine)

Feminine of Albert, from the old English for 'bright and shining'.

Albina

Latin, meaning 'white' or 'fair'.

Alda

German, meaning 'old' or 'prosperous'.

Aldis

English, meaning 'battle-seasoned'.

Aleah

Arabic, meaning 'high', or Persian, meaning 'one of God's beings'.

Aleta

(alt. Aletha)

Greek, meaning 'footloose'.

Alethea

(alt. Aletheia)

Greek, meaning 'truth'.

Alex

(alt. Alexa, Alexi, Alexia, Alexina)

Shortened version of Alexandra, meaning 'man's defender'.

Alexandra

(alt. Alejandra, Alejhandra, Aleksandra, Alessandra, Alexandria)

Feminine of Alexander, from the Greek interpretation of 'man's defender'.

Alexis
(alt. Alexus, Alexys)
Greek, meaning 'helper'.

Aleydis
Variant of Alice, meaning 'nobility'.

Alfreda
Old English, meaning 'elf power'.

Ali
(alt. Allie, Ally)
Shortened version of Alexandra, Aliyah or Alice.

Alibeth
Variant of Elizabeth, meaning 'consecrated to God'.

Alice
(alt. Alize, Alyce, Alys, Alyse)
English, meaning 'noble' or 'nobility'.

Alicia
(alt. Ahlicia, Alecia, Alesia, Alessia, Alizia, Alycia, Alysia)
Variant of Alice, meaning 'nobility'.

Alida
(alt. Aleida)
Latin, meaning 'small winged one'.

Alienor
(alt. Aliana)
Variant spelling of Eleanor, from the Greek for 'light'.

Aliki
(alt. Alika)
Variant of Alice, meaning 'nobility'.

Alima
Arabic, meaning 'cultured'.

Alina
(alt. Alena)
Slavic variation of Helen, meaning 'light'.

Alisha
(alt. Alesha, Alysha)
Variant of Alice, meaning 'nobility'.

Alison
(alt. Allison, Allisyn, Allyson, Alyson)
Variant of Alice, meaning 'nobility'.

Alissa
(alt. Alessa, Alise)

Greek, meaning 'pretty'.

Alivia

Variant spelling of Olivia, meaning 'olive tree'.

Aliya
(alt. Aaliyah, Aleah, Alia, Aliah, Aliyah)

Arabic, meaning 'exalted' or 'sublime'.

Alla

Variant of Ella or Alexandra. Also a possible reference to Allah.

Allegra

Italian, meaning 'joyous'.

Allura

From the French word for entice, meaning 'the power of attraction'.

Allyn

Feminine of Alan, meaning 'peaceful'.

Alma

Three possible origins: Latin for 'giving nurture', Italian for 'soul' and Arabic for 'learned'.

Almeda
(alt. Almeta)

Latin, meaning 'ambitious'.

Almera
(alt. Almira)

Feminine of Elmer, from the Arabic for 'aristocratic'.

Alohi

Variant of the Hawaiian greeting Aloha, meaning 'love and affection'.

Alona

Hebrew, meaning 'oak tree'.

Alora

Variant of Alona, meaning 'oak tree'.

Alpha

The first letter of the Greek alphabet, usually given to a first-born daughter.

Alta

Latin, meaning 'elevated'.

Altagracia

Spanish, meaning 'grace'.

Althea

(alt. Altea, Altha)

Greek, meaning 'healing power'.

Alva

Spanish, meaning 'blonde' or 'fair skinned'.

Alvena

(alt. Alvina)

English, meaning 'noble friend'.

Alvia

(alt. Alyvia)

Variant of Olivia, meaning 'olive tree' or Elvira from the ancient Spanish city.

Alyssa

(alt. Alisa, Alissa, Allyssa, Alysa)

Greek, meaning 'rational'.

Amabel

Variant of Annabel, meaning 'grace and beauty'.

Amadea

Feminine of Amadeus, meaning 'God's beloved'.

Amalia

Variant of Emilia, meaning 'industrious'.

Amana

Hebrew, meaning 'loyal and true'.

Amanda

Latin, meaning 'much loved'.

Amandine

Variant of Amanda, meaning 'much loved'.

Amara

(alt. Amani)

Greek, meaning 'lovely forever'.

Amarantha

Contraction of Amanda and Samantha, meaning 'much loved listener'.

Amaris

(alt. Amari, Amasa, Amata, Amaya)

Hebrew, meaning 'pledged by God'.

Amaryllis

Greek, meaning 'fresh'. Also a flower by the same name.

Amber

From the French word for the semi-precious stone of the same name.

Amberly

Contraction of Amber and Leigh, meaning 'stone' and 'meadow'.

Amberlynn

Contraction of Amber and Lynn, meaning 'stone' and 'waterfall'.

Amboree
(alt. Amber, Ambree)

American, meaning 'precocious'.

Amelia
(alt. Aemilia)

Greek, meaning 'industrious'.

Amelie
(alt. Amalie)

French version of Amelia, meaning 'industrious'.

America

From the country of the same name.

Ameris

Variant of Amaryllis, meaning 'fresh'.

Amethyst

From the Greek word for the precious, mulberry coloured stone of the same name.

Amina

Arabic, meaning 'honest and trustworthy'.

Amira
(alt. Amiya, Amiyah)

Arabic, meaning 'a highborn girl'.

Amity

Latin, meaning 'friendship and harmony'.

Amory

Variant of the Spanish name Amor, meaning 'love'.

Amy
(alt. Amee, Ami, Amie, Ammie)

Latin, meaning 'beloved'.

Amya

Variant of Amy, meaning 'beloved'.

Ana-Lisa

Contraction of Anna and Lisa, meaning 'gracious' or 'consecrated to God'.

Anafa

Hebrew, meaning 'heron'.

Ananda

Hindi, meaning 'bliss'.

Anastasia

(alt. Athanasia)

Greek, meaning 'resurrection'.

Anatolia

From the eastern Greek town of the same name.

Andelyn

Contraction of the feminine for Andrew and Lynn, meaning 'strong waterfall'.

Andrea

(alt. Andreia, Andria)

Feminine of Andrew, from the Greek term for 'a man's woman'.

Andrine

Variant of Andrea, meaning 'a man's woman'.

Andromeda

From the heroine of a Greek legend.

Anemone

Greek, meaning 'breath'.

Angela

(alt. Angel, Angeles, Angelia Angelle, Angie)

Greek, meaning 'messenger from God' or 'angel'.

Angelica

(alt. Angelina, Angeline, Angelique, Angelise, Angelita, Anjelica)

Latin, meaning 'angelic'.

Anise

(alt. Anisa, Anissa)

From the licorice flavoured plant of the same name.

Anita

(alt. Anitra)

Variant of Ann, meaning 'grace'.

Ann

(alt. Anne, Annie)

Derived from Hannah, meaning 'grace'.

A

Anna
(alt. Ana)

Derived from Hannah, meaning 'grace'.

Annabel
(alt. Anabel, Anabelle, Annabell, Annabella, Annabelle)

Contraction of Anna and Belle, meaning 'grace' and 'beauty'.

Annalise
(alt. Annalee, Annaliese, Annalisa, Anneli, Annelie, Annelies, Annelise)

Contraction of Anna and Lise, meaning 'grace' and 'pledged to God'.

Annemarie
(alt. Annamae, Annamarie, Annelle, Annmarie)

Contraction of Anna and Mary, meaning 'grace' and 'bitterness or rebellious'.

Annette
(alt. Annetta)

Derived from Anna and Hannah, meaning 'grace'.

Annis

Greek, meaning 'finished or completed'.

Annora

Latin, meaning 'honour'.

Anoushka
(alt. Anousha)

Russian variant of Ann, meaning 'grace'.

Ansley

English, meaning 'the awesome one's meadow'.

Anthea
(alt. Anthi)

Greek, meaning 'flowerlike'.

Antigone

In Greek mythology, Antigone was the daughter of Oedipus.

Antoinette
(alt. Anonetta, Antonette, Antonietta)

Both a variation of Ann and the feminine of Anthony, meaning 'invaluable grace'.

Antonia
(alt. Antonella, Antonina)

Latin, meaning 'invaluable'.

Anwen

Welsh, meaning 'very fair'.

A

Anya

(alt. Aniya, Aniyah, Aniylah, Anja)

Russian, meaning 'grace'.

Apollonia

Feminine of Apollo, the Greek god of the sun.

Apple

From the name of the fruit.

April

(alt. Avril)

Latin, meaning 'opening up'. Also the name of the month.

Aquilina

(alt. Aqua, Aquila)

Spanish, meaning 'like an eagle'.

Ara

Arabic, meaning 'brings rain'.

Arabella

Latin, meaning 'answered prayer'.

Araceli

(alt. Aracely)

Spanish, meaning 'altar of Heaven'.

Araminta

Contraction of Arabella and Amita, meaning 'altar of Heaven' and 'friendship'.

Araylia

(alt. Araelea)

Latin, meaning 'golden'.

Arcadia

Greek, meaning 'paradise'.

Ardelle

(alt. Ardell, Ardella)

Latin, meaning 'burning with enthusiasm'.

Arden

(alt. Ardis, Ardith)

Latin, meaning 'burning with enthusiasm'.

Arella

(alt. Areli, Arely)

Hebrew, meaning 'angel'.

Aretha

Greek, meaning 'woman of virtue'.

Aria

(alt. Ariah)

Italian, meaning 'melody'.

Ariadne

In Greek mythology, Ariadne was the daughter of King Minos.

Ariana
(alt. Ariane, Arianna, Arienne)

Welsh, meaning 'silver'.

Ariel
(alt. Ariela, Ariella, Arielle)

Hebrew, meaning 'lioness of God'. One of the archangels.

Arlene
(alt. Arleen, Arlie, Arline, Arly)

Gaelic, meaning 'pledge'.

Armida

Latin, meaning 'little armed one'.

Artemisia
(alt. Artemis)

Of both Greek and Spanish origin, meaning 'perfect'.

Artie
(alt. Arti)

Shortened form of Artemisia, meaning 'perfect'.

Ashanti

From the geographical area in Ghana, Africa.

Ashby

English, meaning 'ash tree farm'. Also name of place in Leicestershire.

Ashley
(alt. Ashely, Ashlee, Ashleigh, Ashli, Ashlie, Ashly)

English, meaning 'ash tree meadow'.

Ashlynn
(alt. Ashlyn)

Irish Gaelic, meaning 'dream'.

Ashton
(alt. Ashtyn)

From the place name.

Asia

From the name of continent.

Asma
(alt. Asmara)

Arabic, meaning 'high-standing'.

Aspen
(alt. Aspynn)

From the name of the tree. Also name of a city in the USA.

Assumpta
(alt. Assunta)

Italian, meaning 'raised up'.

Asta
(alt. Asteria, Astor, Astoria)

Greek or Latin, meaning 'star-like'.

Astrid

Old Norse, meaning 'beautiful like a God'.

Atara

Hebrew, meaning 'diadem'.

Athena
(alt. Athenais)

Greek, meaning 'wise'. From the Greek goddess of wisdom.

Aubrey
(alt. Aubree, Aubriana, Aubrie)

French, meaning 'elf ruler'.

Audrey
(alt. Audra, Audrie, Audrina, Audry, Autry)

English, meaning 'noble strength'.

Audrina

Alternative for Audrey, meaning 'noble strength'.

Augusta
(alt. August, Augustine)

Latin, meaning 'worthy of respect'.

Aura
(alt. Aurea)

Greek or Latin, meaning either 'soft breeze' or 'gold'.

Aurelia
(alt. Aurelie)

Latin, meaning 'gold'.

Aurora
(alt. Aurore)

Latin, meaning 'dawn'. In Roman mythology, Aurora was the goddess of sunrise.

Austine
(alt. Austen, Austin)
Latin, meaning 'worthy of respect'.

Autumn
From the name of the season

Ava
(alt. Avia, Avie)
Latin, meaning 'like a bird'.

Avalon
(alt. Avalyn, Aveline)
Celtic, meaning 'island of apples'.

Axelle
Greek, meaning 'father of peace'.

Aya
(alt. Ayah)
Hebrew, meaning 'bird'.

Ayanna
(alt. Ayana)
American, meaning 'grace'.

Ayesha
(alt. Aisha, Aysha)
Persian, meaning 'small one'.

Azalea
Latin, meaning 'dry earth'.

Azalia
Hebrew, meaning 'aided by God'.

Aziza
Hebrew, meaning 'mighty', or Arabic, meaning 'precious'.

Azure
(alt. Azaria)
French, meaning 'sky-blue'.

Popular French names for boys and girls
Alain
Brigitte
Collette
Didier
Fleur
Guillaume
Madeleine
Nadine
Odette
Paulette
Pierre
Thierry

B Girls' names

Babette

French version of Barbara, from the Greek word meaning 'foreign'.

Badia
(alt. Badiyn, Badea)

Arabic, meaning 'elegant'.

Bailey
(alt. Baeli, Bailee)

English, meaning 'law enforcer'.

Bambi

Shortened version of the Italian Bambina, meaning 'child'.

Barbara
(alt. Barb, Barbie, Barbra)

Greek, meaning 'foreign'.

Basma

Arabic, meaning 'smile'.

Bathsheba

Hebrew, meaning 'daughter of the oath'.

Bay
(alt. Baya)

From the plant or geographical name.

Beata

Latin, meaning 'blessed'.

Beatrice
(alt. Beatrix, Beatriz, Bellatrix, Betrys)

Latin, meaning 'bringer of gladness'.

Literary names

Alice (*Alice in Wonderland*, Lewis Carroll)
Bella (*Twilight* novels, Stephanie Meyer)
Charlotte (*The Sorrows of Young Werther*, J. W. von Goethe)
Emma (*Madame Bovary*, Gustave Flaubert)
Esther (*Bleak House*, Charles Dickens)
Iris (*The Blind Assassin*, Margaret Atwood)
Hermione (*Harry Potter* series, J K Rowling)
Matilda (*Matilda*, Roald Dahl)
Shirley (*Shirley*, Charlotte Brontë)
Wendy (*Peter Pan*, J M Barrie)

Becky
(*alt. Beccie, Beccy, Beckie*)
Shortened form of Rebecca, meaning 'noose'.

Bee
Shortened form of Beatrice, meaning 'bringer of gladness'.

Belinda
(*alt. Belen, Belina*)
Contraction of Belle and Linda, meaning 'beautiful'.

Bell
Shortened form of Isabel, meaning 'pledged to God'.

Bella
Latin, meaning 'beautiful'.

Belle
French, meaning 'beautiful'.

Belva
Latin, meaning 'beautiful view'.

Bénédicta
Latin, the feminine of Benedict, meaning 'blessed'.

Benita
(*alt. Bernita*)
Spanish, meaning 'blessed'.

Bennie
Shortened version of Bénédicta and Benita, meaning 'blessed'.

B

Berit

(alt. Beret)

Scandinavian, meaning 'splendid' or 'gorgeous'.

Bernadette

French, meaning 'courageous'.

Bernadine

French, meaning 'courageous'.

Bernice

(alt. Berenice, Berniece, Burnice)

Greek, meaning 'she who brings victory'.

Bertha

(alt. Berta, Berthe, Bertie)

German, meaning 'bright'.

Beryl

Greek, meaning 'pale green gemstone'.

Bess

(alt. Bessie)

Shortened form of Elizabeth, meaning 'consecrated to God'.

Beth

Hebrew, meaning 'house'. Also shortened form of Elizabeth, meaning 'consecrated to God'.

Bethany

(alt. Bethan)

Biblical, referring to a geographical location.

Bethel

Hebrew, meaning 'house of God'.

Bettina

Spanish version of Elizabeth, meaning 'consecrated to God'.

Betty

(alt. Betsy, Bette, Bettie, Bettye)

Shortened version of Elizabeth, meaning 'consecrated to God'.

Beulah

Hebrew, meaning 'married'.

Beverly

(alt. Beverlee, Beverley)

English, meaning 'beaver stream'.

Bevin

Celtic, meaning 'fair lady'.

B

Beyoncé

American, made popular by the singer.

Bianca

(alt. Blanca)

Italian, meaning 'white'.

Bibiana

Greek, meaning 'alive'.

Bijou

French, meaning 'jewel'.

Billie

(alt. Bill, Billy, Billye)

Shortened version of Wilhelmina, meaning 'determined'.

Bina

Hebrew, meaning 'knowledge'.

Birgit

(alt. Birgitta)

Norwegian, meaning 'splendid'.

Blair

Scottish Gaelic, meaning 'flat, plain area'.

Blake

(alt. Blakely, Blakelyn)

English, meaning either 'pale-skinned' or 'dark'.

Blanche

(alt. Blanch)

French, meaning 'white or pale'.

Bliss

English, meaning 'intense happiness'.

Blithe

English, meaning 'joyous'.

Blodwen

Welsh, meaning 'white flower'.

Blossom

English, meaning 'flowerlike'.

Blythe

(alt. Bly)

English, meaning 'happy and carefree'.

Bobbi

(alt. Bobbie, Bobby)

Shortened version of Roberta, meaning 'famous brilliance'.

Bonamy
(alt. Bomani, Bonamia, Bonamea)

French, meaning 'close friend'.

Bonita
Spanish, meaning 'pretty'.

Bonnie
(alt. Bonny)

Scottish, meaning 'fair of face'.

Brandy
(alt. Brandee, Brandi, Brandie)

From the name of the liquor.

Branwen
Welsh, meaning 'a white crow'.

Brea
(alt. Bree, Bria)

Shortened form of Brianna, meaning 'strong'.

Brenda
Old Norse, meaning 'sword'.

Brianna
(alt. Breana, Breanna, Breanne)

Irish Gaelic, meaning 'strong'.

Bridget
(alt. Bridgett, Bridgette, Brigette, Brigid, Brigitta, Brigitte)

Irish Gaelic, meaning 'strength and power'.

Brier
French, meaning 'heather'.

Brit
(alt. Britt, Britta)

Celtic, meaning 'spotted' or 'freckled'.

Biblical names

Abigail
Delilah
Eve
Hannah
Mary
Naomi
Rebecca
Ruth
Sarah
Salome

B

Britannia

Latin, meaning 'Britain'.

Brittany

(alt. Britany, Britney, Britni, Brittani, Brittanie, Brittney, Brittni, Brittny)

Latin, meaning 'from England'.

Bronwyn

(alt. Bronwen)

Welsh, meaning 'fair breast'.

Brooke

(alt. Brook)

English, meaning 'small stream'.

Brooklyn

(alt. Brooklynn)

From the name of a New York borough.

Brunhilda

German, meaning 'armour-wearing fighting maid'.

Bryn

(alt. Brynn)

Welsh, meaning 'mount'.

Bryony

(alt. Briony)

From the name of a European vine.

Buffy

American alternative of Elizabeth, meaning 'consecrated to God'.

Popular Indian names for boys and girls

Anjali
Bharat
Deepal
Haresh
Jamal
Jaya
Manisha
Naima
Nikhil
Paresh
Ravi
Shreya
Talan

B

C Girls' names

Cadew
French, meaning 'gift'.

Cadence
Latin, meaning 'with rhythm'.

Cai
Vietnamese, meaning 'feminine'.

Caitlin
(alt. Cadyn, Caitlann, Caitlyn, Caitlynn)
Greek, meaning 'pure'.

Calandra
Greek, meaning 'lark'.

Calantha
(alt. Calanthe)
Greek, meaning 'lovely flower'.

Caledonia
Latin, meaning 'from Scotland'.

Calia
American, meaning 'renowned beauty'.

Calla
Greek, meaning 'beautiful'.

Callie
(alt. Caleigh, Cali, Calleigh, Cally)
Greek, meaning 'beauty'.

Calliope
From the muse of epic poetry in Greek mythology.

Callista
(alt. Callisto)
Greek, meaning 'most beautiful'.

227

Camas

Native American, from the root and bulb of the same name.

Cambria

Welsh, from the alternative name of the same country.

Camden
(alt. Camdyn)

English, meaning 'winding valley'.

Cameo

Italian, meaning 'skin'.

Cameron
(alt. Camryn)

Scottish Gaelic, meaning 'bent nose'.

Camilla
(alt. Camelia, Camellia, Camila, Camillia)

Latin, meaning 'spiritual serving girl'.

Camille

Latin, meaning 'spiritual serving girl'.

Candace
(alt. Candice, Candis)

Latin, meaning 'brilliant white'.

Candida

Latin, meaning 'white'.

Candra

Latin, meaning 'glowing'.

Candy
(alt. Candi)

Shortened form of Candace, meaning 'brilliant white'.

Canei

Greek, meaning 'pure'.

Caoimhe

Celtic, meaning 'gentleness'.

Caprice

Italian, meaning 'ruled by whim'.

Cara

Latin, meaning 'darling'.

Caren
(alt. Carin, Caron, Caryn)

Greek, meaning 'pure'.

Carey

(alt. Cari, Carie, Carri, Carrie, Cary)

Welsh, meaning 'near the castle'.

Carina

(alt. Corina)

Italian, meaning 'dearest little one'.

Carissa

(alt. Carisa)

Greek, meaning 'grace'.

Carla

(alt. Charla)

Feminine of the German Carl, meaning 'man'.

Carlin

(alt. Carleen, Carlene)

Gaelic, meaning 'little champion'.

Carlotta

(alt. Carlota)

Italian variant of 'Charlotte', meaning 'little and feminine'.

Carly

(alt. Carlee, Carley, Carli, Carlie)

Feminine of the German Charles, meaning 'man'.

Carmel

(alt. Carmela, Carmelita, Carmella)

Hebrew, meaning 'garden'.

Carmen

(alt. Carma, Carmina)

Latin, meaning 'song'.

Carol

(alt. Carole, Carrol, Carroll, Caryl)

Shortened form of Caroline, meaning 'man'.

Caroline

(alt. Carolann, Carolina, Carolyn, Carolynn)

German, meaning 'man'.

Carrington

English, meaning 'Charles's town'.

Carys

(alt. Cerys)

Welsh, meaning 'love'.

Casey

Irish Gaelic, meaning 'watchful'.

C

Saints' names

Agatha
Agnes
Barbara
Cecilia
Genevieve
Louise
Matilda
Seraphina
Tatiana
Teresa
Vivian

Cassandra
(alt. Casandra, Cassandre)
Greek, meaning 'one who prophesies doom'.

Cassia
(alt. Casia, Casie, Cassie)
Greek, meaning 'cinnamon'.

Cassidy
Irish, meaning 'clever'.

Cassiopeia
(alt. Cassiopia, Cassiopea)
From the constellation and the Greek myth.

Catalina
(alt. Catarina, Caterina)
Spanish version of Catherine, meaning 'pure'.

Catherine
(alt. Catharine, Cathrine, Cathryn)
Greek, meaning 'pure'.

Cathleen
Irish version of Catherine, meaning 'pure'.

Cathy
(alt. Cathey, Cathi, Cathie)
Shortened form of Catherine, meaning 'pure'.

Caty
(alt. Caddie, Caitee, Cate, Catie)
Shortened form of Catherine, meaning 'pure'.

Cayley
(alt. Cayla, Caylee, Caylen)
American, meaning 'pure'.

Cecilia
(alt. Cecelia, Cecily, Cicely, Cicily)
Latin, meaning 'blind one'.

C

Cecile
(alt. Cecilie)

Latin, meaning 'blind one'.

Celena

Greek, meaning 'goddess of the moon'.

Celeste
(alt. Celestina, Celestine)

Latin, meaning 'heavenly'.

Celine
(alt. Celia, Celina)

French version of Celeste, meaning 'heavenly'.

Cerise

French, meaning 'cherry'.

Chanah

Hebrew, meaning 'grace'.

Chandler
(alt. Chandell)

English, meaning 'candle maker'.

Chandra
(alt. Chanda, Chandry)

Sanskrit, meaning 'like the moon'.

Chanel
(alt. Chanelle)

French, meaning 'pipe'. Most often associated with the designer of the same name.

Chantal
(alt. Chantel, Chantelle, Chantilly)

French, meaning 'stony spot'.

Chardonnay

French, from the wine variety of the same name.

Charis
(alt. Charissa, Charisse)

Greek, meaning 'grace'.

Charity

Latin, meaning 'brotherly love'.

Charlene
(alt. Charleen, Charline)

German, meaning 'man'.

Charlie
(alt. Charlee, Charley Charlize, Charly)

Shortened form of Charlotte, meaning 'little and feminine'.

C

Charlotte
(alt. Charnette, Charolette)
French, meaning 'little and feminine'.

Charmaine
Latin, meaning 'clan'.

Charnelle
(alt. Charnell, Charnel, Charnele)
American, meaning 'sparkles'.

Chastity
Latin, meaning 'purity'.

Chava
(alt. Chaya)
Hebrew, meaning 'beloved'.

Chelsea
(alt. Chelsee, Chelsey, Chelsi, Chelsie)
English, meaning 'port or landing place'.

Cher
French, meaning 'beloved'. Most often associated with the singer of the same name.

Cherie
(alt. Cheri, Cherise)
French, meaning 'dear'.

Cherish
(alt. Cherith)
English, meaning 'to treasure'.

Ciara
Irish, meaning 'dark beauty'.

Chermona
Hebrew, meaning 'sacred mountain'.

Cherry
(alt. Cherri)
French, meaning 'cherry fruit'.

TV personality names

Alexa (Chung)
Arlene (Phillips)
Davina (McCall)
Janet (Street-Porter)
Kirsty (Gallacher)
Lauren (Laverne)
Myleene (Klass)
Natasha (Kaplinsky)
Tess (Daly)
Trisha (Goddard)

Cheryl
(alt. Cheryle)

English, meaning 'little and womanly'.

Chesney

English, meaning 'place to camp'.

Cheyenne
(alt. Cheyanne)

Native American, from the tribe of the same name.

Chiara
(alt. Ceara, Chiarina, Ciara)

Italian, meaning 'light'.

China

From the country of the same name.

Chiquita

Spanish, meaning 'little one'.

Chloe
(alt. Cloe)

Greek, meaning 'pale green shoot'.

Chloris

Greek, meaning 'pale'.

Chris
(alt. Chrissy, Christa, Christie, Christy, Crissy, Cristy)

Shortened form of Christina, meaning 'anointed Christian'.

Christabel

Both Latin and French, meaning 'fair Christian'. The title of a poem by Coleridge.

Christina
(alt. Christiana, Cristina)

Greek, meaning 'anointed Christian'.

Christine
(alt. Christeen, Christene, Christiane, Christin)

Greek, meaning 'anointed Christian'.

Chuma

Aramaic, meaning 'warmth'.

Ciara

Irish, meaning 'dark beauty'.

Cierra
(alt. Ciera)

Irish, meaning 'black'.

Cinderella

French, meaning 'little ash-girl'. Most often associated with the fairytale.

Cindy

(alt. Cinda, Cindi, Cyndi)

Shortened form of Cynthia, meaning 'goddess'.

Cinnamon

Greek, from the spice of the same name.

Citlali

(alt. Citlalli)

Aztec, meaning 'star'.

Citrine

Latin, from the gemstone of the same name.

Claire

(alt. Clare)

Latin, meaning 'bright'.

Clara

(alt. Claira)

Latin, meaning 'bright'.

Clarabelle

(alt. Claribel)

Contraction of Clara and Isobel, meaning 'bright' and 'consecrated to God'.

Clarissa

(alt. Clarice, Clarisse)

Variation of Claire, meaning 'bright'.

Clarity

Latin, meaning 'lucid'.

Claudette

Latin, meaning 'lame'.

Claudia

(alt. Claudie, Claudine)

Latin, meaning 'lame'.

Clematis

Greek, meaning 'vine'.

Clementine

(alt. Clemency, Clementina, Clemmie)

Latin, meaning 'mild and merciful'.

Cleopatra

Greek, meaning 'her father's renown'. Most often associated with the Egyptian queen.

C

Clio

(alt. Cleo, Cliona)

Greek, from the muse of history of the same name.

Clodagh

Irish, meaning 'river'.

Clotilda

(alt. Clothilda, Clothilde, Clotilde)

German, meaning 'renowned battle'.

Clover

English, from the flower of the same name.

Cloud

American, meaning 'lighthearted'.

Coco

Spanish, meaning 'help'.

Cody

English, meaning 'pillow'.

Colleen

(alt. Coleen)

Irish Gaelic, meaning 'girl'.

Collette

(alt. Colette)

Greek and French, meaning 'people of victory'.

Connie

Latin, meaning 'steadfast'.

Constance

(alt. Constanza)

Latin, meaning 'steadfast'.

Consuelo

(alt. Consuela)

Spanish, meaning 'comfort'.

Cora

Greek, meaning 'maiden'.

Coral

(alt. Coralie, Coraline, Corelia, Corene)

Latin, from the marine life of the same name.

Corazon

Spanish, meaning 'heart'.

Cordelia

(alt. Cordia, Cordie)

Latin, meaning 'heart'.

C

Corey
(alt. Cori, Corrie, Cory)
Irish Gaelic, meaning 'the hollow'.

Corin
(alt. Corine)
Latin, meaning 'spear'.

Corinne
(alt. Corinna, Corrine)
French version of Cora, meaning 'maiden'.

Corliss
English, meaning 'cheery'.

Cornelia
Latin, meaning 'like a horn'.

Cosette
French, meaning 'people of victory'.

Cosima
(alt. Cosmina)
Greek, meaning 'order'.

Courtney
(alt. Cortney)
English, meaning 'court-dweller'.

Creola
French, meaning 'American-born, English descent'.

Crescent
French, meaning 'increasing'.

Cressida
From the heroine in Greek mythology of the same name.

Crystal
(alt. Christal, Chrystal, Cristal)
Greek, meaning 'ice'.

Csilla
Hungarian, meaning 'defences'.

Cynara
Greek, meaning 'thistly plant'.

Cynthia
Greek, meaning 'goddess from the mountain'.

Cyra
Persian, meaning 'sun'.

Cyrilla
Latin, meaning 'lordly'.

C

 # Girls' names

Dacey

Irish Gaelic, meaning 'from the south'.

Dada

Nigerian, meaning 'curly haired'.

Daelan

English, meaning 'aware'.

Dagmar

German, meaning 'day's glory'.

Dagny

Nordic, meaning 'new day'.

Dahlia

Scandinavian, from the flower of the same name.

Dai

Japanese, meaning 'great'.

Daisy
(alt. Dasia)

English, meaning 'eye of the day'.

Dakota

Native American, meaning 'allies'.

Dalia
(alt. Dalila)

Hebrew, meaning 'delicate branch'.

Dallas

Scottish Gaelic, from the village of the same name. Also city in America.

Damaris

Greek, meaning 'calf'.

Damica

(alt. Damika)

French, meaning 'friendly'.

Damita

Spanish, meaning 'little noblewoman'.

Dana

(alt. Dania, Danna, Dayna)

English, meaning 'from Denmark'.

Danae

Greek, from the mythological heroine of the same name.

Danica

(alt. Danika)

Latin, meaning 'from Denmark'.

Danielle

(alt. Danelle, Daniela, Daniella, Danila, Danyelle)

The feminine form of the Hebrew Daniel, meaning 'God is my judge'.

Danita

English, meaning 'God will judge'.

Daphne

(alt. Dafne, Daphna)

Of Greek origin, meaning 'laurel tree'.

Dara

Hebrew and Persian, meaning 'wisdom'.

Darby

(alt. Darbi, Darbie)

Irish, meaning 'park with deer'.

Darcie

(alt. Darci, Darcy)

Irish Gaelic, meaning 'dark'.

Daria

Greek, meaning 'rich'.

Darla

English, meaning 'darling'.

Darlene

(alt. Darleen, Darline)

American, meaning 'darling'.

Darva

Slavic, meaning 'honeybee'.

Daryl
(alt. Darryl)

English, originally used as a surname. Often associated with the actress Daryl Hannah.

Davina

Hebrew, meaning 'loved one'. Best known for the TV presenter Davina McCall.

Dawn
(alt. Dawna)

English, meaning 'the dawn'.

Daya

Hebrew, meaning 'bird of prey'.

Deanna
(alt. Dayana, Deana, Deanna, Deanne)

English, meaning 'valley'.

Debbie
(alt. Debbi, Debby, Debi)

Shortened form of Deborah, meaning 'bee'.

Deborah
(alt. Debbra, Debora, Debra, Debrah)

Hebrew, meaning 'bee'.

December

Latin, meaning 'tenth month'.

Decima
(alt. Decia)

Latin, meaning 'tenth'.

Dee

Welsh, meaning 'swarthy'.

Deidre
(alt. Deidra, Deirdre)

Irish, meaning 'raging woman'.

Deja
(alt. Dejah)

French, meaning 'already'.

Delaney

Irish Gaelic, meaning 'offspring of the challenger'.

Delia

Greek, meaning 'from Delos'.

Delilah
(alt. Delina)

Hebrew, meaning 'seductive'.

Della
(alt. Dell)

Shortened form of Adele, meaning 'nobility'.

D

Delores
(alt. Deloris)
Spanish, meaning 'sorrows'.

Delphine
(alt. Delpha, Delphia, Delphina, Delphinia)
Greek, meaning 'dolphin'.

Delta
Greek, meaning 'fourth child'.

Demetria
(alt. Demetrice)
Greek, from the mythological heroine of the same name.

Demi
French, meaning 'half'. Best known for the actress Demi Moore.

Dena
(alt. Deena)
English, meaning 'from the valley'.

Denise
(alt. Denice, Denisa, Denisse)
French, meaning 'follower of Dionysius'.

Derora
Hebrew, meaning 'stream'.

Desdemona
Greek, meaning 'wretchedness'.

Desiree
(alt. Desirae)
French, meaning 'much desired'.

Desma
Greek, meaning 'blinding oath'.

Destiny
(alt. Destany, Destinee, Destiney, Destini)
French, meaning 'fate'.

Deva
Hindi, meaning 'God-like'.

Devin
(alt. Devinne)
Irish Gaelic, meaning 'poet'.

Devon
English, from the county of the same name.

Diamond
English, meaning 'brilliant'.

Diana
(alt. Dian, Diane, Dianna, Dianne)
Roman, meaning 'divine'.

D

Uncommon three-syllable names

Annabel
Cassandra
Dolores
Gloria
Harriet
Imogen
Julia
Marilyn
Miranda
Nigella

Diandra

Greek, meaning 'two males'.

Dilys

Welsh, meaning 'reliable'.

Dimitra

Greek, meaning 'follower of Demeter'.

Dimona

Hebew, meaning 'south'.

Dinah

(alt. Dina)

Hebew, meaning 'justified'.

Dionne

Greek, from the mythological heroine of the same name.

Divine

Italian, meaning 'heavenly'.

Dixie

French, meaning 'tenth'.

Dodie

Hebew, meaning 'well-loved'.

Dolly

(alt. Dollie)

Shortened form of Dorothy, meaning 'gift of God'.

Dolores

(alt. Doloris)

Spanish, meaning 'sorrows'.

Dominique

(alt. Domenica, Dominica, Domonique)

Latin, meaning 'Lord'.

Donata

Latin, meaning 'given'.

Donna

(alt. Dona, Donnie)

Italian, meaning 'lady'.

D

Dora

Greek, meaning 'gift'.

Dorcas

Greek, meaning 'gazelle'.

Doreen
(alt. Dorene, Dorine)

Irish Gaelic, meaning 'brooding'.

Doria

Greek, meaning 'of the sea'.

Doris
(alt. Dorris)

Greek, from the region of the same name.

Dorothy
(alt. Dorathy, Doretha, Dorotha, Dorothea, Dorthy)

Greek, meaning 'gift of God'.

Dorrit
(alt. Dorit)

Greek, meaning 'gift of God'.

Dory
(alt. Dori)

French, meaning 'gilded'.

Dottie
(alt. Dotty)

Shortened form of Dorothy, meaning 'gift of God'.

Dove
(alt. Dovie)

English, from the bird of the same name.

Drew

Greek, meaning 'masculine'.

Drusilla
(alt. Drucilla)

Latin, meaning 'of the Drusus clan'.

Dulcie
(alt. Dulce, Dulcia)

Latin, meaning 'sweet'.

Dusty
(alt. Dusti)

Old German, meaning 'brave warrior'. Often associated with the singer Dusty Springfield.

D

E Girls' names

Eadlin
(alt. Eadlinn, Eadlyn, Eadlen)
Anglo-Saxon, meaning 'royalty'.

Earla
English, meaning 'leader'.

Eartha
English, meaning 'earth'.

Easter
Egyptian, from the festival of the same name.

Ebba
English, meaning 'fortress of riches'.

Ebony
(alt. Eboni)
Latin, meaning 'deep black wood'.

Echo
Greek, from the mythological nymph of the same name.

Eda
(alt. Edda)
English, meaning 'wealthy and happy'.

Edelmira
Spanish, meaning 'admired for nobility'.

Eden
Hebrew, meaning 'pleasure'.

Edie
(alt. Eddie)
Shortened form of Eden, meaning 'pleasure'.

Edina
Scottish, meaning 'from Edinburgh'.

Edith
(alt. Edyth)
English, meaning 'prosperity through battle'.

Edna
Hebrew, meaning 'enjoyment'.

Edrea
English, meaning 'wealthy and powerful'.

Edris
(alt. Edriss, Edrys)
Anglo-Saxon, meaning 'prosperous ruler'.

Edwina
English, meaning 'wealthy friend'.

Effie
Greek, meaning 'pleasant speech'.

Eglantine
French, from the shrub of the same name.

Eibhlín
Irish Gaelic, meaning 'shining and brilliant'.

Eileen
Irish, meaning 'shining and brilliant'.

Ekaterina
(alt. Ekaterini)
Slavic, meaning 'pure'.

Elaine
(alt. Elaina, Elayne)
French, meaning 'bright, shining light'.

Elba
Italian, from the island of the same name.

Elberta
English, meaning 'highborn'.

Eldora
Spanish, meaning 'covered with gold'.

Eldoris
(alt. Eldoriss, Eldorys)
Greek, meaning 'woman of the sea'.

Eleanor
(alt. Elana, Elanor, Eleanora)
Greek, meaning 'light'.

Electra
(alt. Elektra)

Greek, meaning 'shining'. Also from the myth.

Elfrida
(alt. Elfrieda)

English, meaning 'elf power'.

Eliane

Hebrew, meaning 'Jehovah is God'.

Elissa
(alt. Elisa)

French, meaning 'pledged to God'.

Eliza
(alt. Elisha)

Hebrew, meaning 'consecrated to God'.

Elizabeth
(alt. Elisabet, Elisabeth, Elizabella, Elizabelle, Elsbeth, Elspeth)

Hebrew, meaning 'consecrated to God'.

Elke

German, meaning 'nobility'.

Ella

German, meaning 'completely'.

Ellema
(alt. Ellemah, Elema, Ellemma, Elemah)

African, meaning 'dairy farmer'.

Elle
(alt. Ellie)

French, meaning 'she'.

Ellen
(alt. Elin, Eline, Ellyn)

Greek, meaning 'shining'.

Ellice
(alt. Elyse)

Greek, meaning 'the Lord is God'.

Elma
(alt. Elna)

Latin, meaning 'soul'.

Elmira

Arabic, meaning 'aristocratic lady'.

Elodie

French, meaning 'marsh flower'.

Eloise
(alt. Elois, Eloisa, Elouise)

French, meaning 'renowned in battle'.

Elsa
(alt. Else, Elsie)

Hebrew, meaning 'consecrated to God'.

Elva
Irish, meaning 'noble'.

Elvina
English, meaning 'noble friend'.

Elvira
(alt. Elvera)

Spanish, from the ancient city of the same name.

Ember
(alt. Embry)

English, meaning 'spark'.

Emeline
German, meaning 'industrious'.

Emerald
English, meaning 'green gemstone'.

Emery
German, meaning 'ruler of work'.

Emiko
(alt. Emuko)

Japanese, meaning 'pretty child'.

Emilia
Latin, meaning 'from the Emily clan'.

Emily
(alt. Emalee, Emelie, Emely, Emilee, Emilie, Emlyn)

Latin, from the clan of the same name.

Emma
German, meaning 'embraces everything'. The title character of Jane Austen's novel.

Emmanuelle
Hebrew, meaning 'God is among us'.

Emmeline
(alt. Emmelina)

German, meaning 'embraces everything'.

Emmy
(alt. Emi, Emme, Emmie)

German, meaning 'embraces everything'.

Ena
Shortened form of Georgina, meaning 'farmer'.

Enid
(alt. Eneida)

Welsh, meaning 'life spirit'.

E

Enola

Native American, meaning 'solitary'.

Enya

Irish Gaelic, meaning 'fire'.

Eranthe

Greek, meaning 'delicate like the spring'.

Erica
(alt. Ericka, Erika)

Scandinavian, meaning 'ruler forever'.

Erin
(alt. Eryn)

Irish Gaelic, meaning 'from the isle to the west'.

Eris

Greek, from the mythological heroine of the same name.

Erlinda

Hebrew, meaning 'spirited'.

Erma

German, meaning 'universal'.

Ermine

French, meaning 'weasel'.

Erna

English, meaning 'sincere'.

Ernestine
(alt. Ernestina)

English, meaning 'sincere'.

Esme

French, meaning 'esteemed'.

Esmeralda

Spanish, meaning 'emerald'.

Esperanza

Spanish, meaning 'hope'.

Estelle
(alt. Estela, Estell, Estella)

French, meaning 'star'.

Esther
(alt. Esta, Ester, Etha, Ethna, Ethne)

Persian, meaning 'star'.

Etinia
(alt. Eteniah, Etene, Eteniya)

Native American, meaning 'prosperous'.

Eternity

Latin, meaning 'forever'.

E

Ethel
(alt. Ethyl)
English, meaning 'noble'.

Etta
(alt. Etter, Ettie)
Shortened form of Henrietta, meaning 'ruler of the house'.

Eudora
Greek, meaning 'generous gift'.

Eugenia
(alt. Eugenie)
Greek, meaning 'wellborn'.

Eulalia
(alt. Eula, Eulah, Eulalie)
Greek, meaning 'sweet-speaking'.

Eunice
Greek, meaning 'victorious'.

Euphemia
Greek, meaning ' favourable speech'.

Eva
Hebrew, meaning 'life'.

Evadne
Greek, meaning 'pleasing one'.

Evangeline
(alt. Evangelina)
Greek, meaning 'good news'.

Evanthe
Greek, meaning 'good flower'.

Eve
(alt. Evie)
Hebrew, meaning 'life'. The first woman created by God in the Bible.

Evelina
(alt. Evelia)
German, meaning 'hazelnut'.

Evelyn
(alt. Evalyn, Evelin, Eveline, Evelyne)
German, meaning 'hazelnut'.

Everly
(alt. Everleigh, Everley)
English, meaning 'grazing meadow'.

Evette
French, meaning 'yew wood'.

Evonne
(alt. Evon)
French, meaning 'yew wood'.

E

F Girls' names

Fabia
(alt. Fabiana, Fabienne, Fabiola, Fabriana)
Latin, meaning 'from the Fabian clan'.

Fabrizia
Italian, meaning 'works with hands'.

Fahari
Swahili, meaning 'splendour'.

Faith
English, meaning 'loyalty'.

Faiza
Arabic, meaning 'victorious'.

Fallon
Irish Gaelic, meaning 'descended from a ruler'.

Fanny
(alt Fannie)
Latin, meaning 'from France'.

Farica
German, meaning 'peaceful ruler'.

Farrah
English, meaning 'lovely and pleasant'.

Fatima
Arabic, from the daughter of Mohammed with the same name.

Faustine
Latin, meaning 'fortunate'.

Fawn
French, meaning 'young deer'.

Fay
(alt. Fae, Faye)
French, meaning 'fairy'.

Fayola
(alt. Fayolah, Fayeena)
African, meaning 'walks with honour'.

Felicia
(alt. Felecia, Felice, Felicita, Felisha)
Latin, meaning 'lucky and happy'.

Felicity
Latin, meaning 'fortunate'.

Fenella
Irish Gaelic, meaning 'white shoulder'.

Fenia
Scandinavian, from the mythological giantess of the same name.

Fern
(alt. Ferne, Ferrin)
English, from the plant of the same name.

Fernanda
German, meaning 'peace and courage'.

Ffion
(alt. Fion)
Irish Gaelic, meaning 'fair and pale'.

Old name, new fashion?

Arabella
Clarissa
Clara
Dorothy
Evelyn
Hazel
Marjorie
Nora
Penelope
Rosamond

F

Fia

Italian, meaning 'flame'.

Fifi

Hebrew, meaning 'Jehovah increases'.

Filomena

Greek, meaning 'loved one'.

Finlay
(alt. Finley)

Irish Gaelic, meaning 'fair-headed courageous one'.

Finola
(alt. Fionnula)

Irish Gaelic, meaning 'fair shoulder'.

Fiona

Irish Gaelic, meaning 'fair and pale'.

Fiorella

Italian, meaning 'little flower'.

Fiora

Irish Gaelic, meaning 'fair and pale'.

Flanna
(alt. Flannery)

Irish Gaelic, meaning 'russet hair'.

Flavia

Latin, meaning 'yellow hair'.

Fleur

French, meaning 'flower'.

Flo
(alt. Florrie, Flossie, Floy)

Shortened forms of Florence, meaning 'in bloom'.

Flora

Latin, meaning 'flower'.

Florence
(alt. Florencia, Florene, Florine)

Latin, meaning 'in bloom'. Also the Italian city.

Florida

Latin, meaning 'flowery'. Also a state in America.

Fran
(alt. Frankie, Frannie)

Shortened form of Frances, meaning 'from France'.

F

Frances

(alt. Francine, Francis)

Latin, meaning 'from France'.

Francesca

(alt. Franchesca, Francisca)

Latin, meaning 'from France'.

Freda

(alt. Freeda, Freida, Frida, Frieda)

German, meaning 'peaceful'.

Frederica

German, meaning 'peaceful ruler'.

Fuchsia

German, from the flower of the same name.

Fumik

Japanese, meaning 'little friend'.

Names of poets

Amy (Lowell)
Anne (Sexton)
Carol Ann (Duffy)
Charlotte (Smith)
Emily (Dickinson)
Fleur (Adcock)
Gwyneth (Lewis)
Ruth (Padel)
Pam (Ayres)
Sylvia (Plath)
Wendy (Cope)

F

Girls' names

Gabby
(alt. Gabbi)

Shortened form of Gabrielle, meaning 'heroine of God'.

Gabrielle
(alt. Gabriel, Gabriela, Gabriella)

Hebrew, meaning 'heroine of God'.

Gadara

Armenian, meaning 'mountain's peak'.

Gaia
(alt. Gaea)

Greek, meaning 'the earth'.

Gail
(alt. Gale, Gayla, Gayle)

Hebrew, meaning 'my father rejoices'.

Gala

French, meaning 'festive merrymaking'.

Galiena

German, meaning 'high one'.

Galina

Russian, meaning 'shining brightly'.

Garnet
(alt. Garnett)

English, meaning 'red gemstone'.

Gay
(alt. Gaye)

French, meaning 'glad and lighthearted'.

Gaynor

Welsh, meaning 'white and smooth'.

Gemini

Greek, meaning 'twin'. One of the signs of the zodiac.

Gemma

Italian, meaning 'precious stone'.

Gene

Greek, meaning 'wellborn'.

Genesis

Greek, meaning 'beginning'.

Geneva
(alt. Genevra)

French, meaning 'juniper tree'.

Genevieve

German, meaning 'white wave'.

Genie

Shortened form of Genevieve, meaning 'white wave'.

Georgette

French, meaning 'farmer'.

Names from ancient Rome

Agnes
Cecilia
Chloris
Diana
Flavia
Lavinia
Octavia
Paula
Portia
Tatiana

Georgia
(alt. Georgiana, Georgianna, Georgie)

Latin, meaning 'farmer'.

Georgina
(alt. Georgene, Georgine, Giorgina)

Latin, meaning 'farmer'.

Geraldine

German, meaning 'spear ruler'.

Gerda

Nordic, meaning 'shelter'.

G

Geri

(alt. Gerri, Gerry)

Shortened form of Geraldine, meaning 'spear ruler'.

Germaine

French, meaning 'from Germany'.

Gertie

Shortened form of Gertrude, meaning 'strength of a spear'.

Gertrude

German, meaning 'strength of a spear'.

Ghislaine

French, meaning 'pledge'.

Gia

(alt. Ghia)

Italian, meaning 'God is gracious'.

Gianina

(alt. Giana)

Hebrew, meaning 'God's graciousness'.

Gigi

(alt. Giget)

Shortened form of Georgina, meaning 'farmer'.

Gilda

English, meaning 'gilded'.

Gilia

Hebrew, meaning 'joy of the Lord'.

Gillian

Latin, meaning 'youthful'.

Gina

(alt. Geena, Gena)

Shortened form of Regina, meaning 'queen'.

Ginger

Latin, from the root of the same name.

Ginny

Shortened form of Virginia, meaning 'virgin'.

Giovanna

Italian, meaning 'God is gracious'.

Giselle

(alt. Gisela, Gisele, Giselle, Gisselle)

German, meaning 'pledge'.

G

Gita
(alt. Geeta)

Sanskrit, meaning 'song'.

Giulia
(alt. Giuliana)

Italian, meaning 'youthful'.

Gladys
(alt. Gladyce)

Welsh, meaning 'lame'.

Glenda

Welsh, meaning 'fair and good'.

Glenna
(alt. Glennie)

Irish Gaelic, meaning 'glen'.

Glenys

Welsh, meaning 'riverbank'.

Gloria
(alt. Glory)

Latin, meaning 'glory'.

Glynda
(alt. Glinda)

Welsh, meaning 'fair'. The good witch in the *Wizard of Oz*.

Glynis

Welsh, meaning 'small glen'.

Golda
(alt. Goldia, Goldie)

English, meaning 'gold'.

Grace
(alt. Graça, Gracie, Gracin, Grayce)

Latin, meaning 'grace'.

Grainne
(alt. Grania)

Irish Gaelic, meaning 'love'.

Gratia
(alt. Grasia)

Latin, meaning 'blessing'.

Greer
(alt. Grier)

Latin, meaning 'alert and watchful'.

Gregoria

Latin, meaning 'alert'.

Greta
(alt. Gretel)

Greek, meaning 'pearl'.

Gretchen

German, meaning 'pearl'.

Griselda

(alt. Griselle)

German, meaning 'grey fighting maid'.

Gudrun

Scandinavian, meaning 'battle'.

Guinevere

Welsh, meaning 'white and smooth'. The queen in Arthurian legend.

Gwen

Shortened form of Gwendolyn, meaning 'fair bow'.

Gwenda

Welsh, meaning 'fair and good'.

Gwendolyn

(alt. Gwendolen, Gwenel)

Welsh, meaning 'fair bow'.

Gwynn

(alt. Gwyn)

Welsh, meaning 'fair blessed'.

Gwyneth

(alt. Gwynneth, Gwynyth)

Welsh, meaning 'happiness'.

Gypsy

English, meaning 'of the Roman tribe'.

Grythao

English, meaning 'fiery'.

Names from ancient Greece

Agatha
Ariadne
Berenice
Cressida
Iliana
Lisandra
Medea
Nereida
Sophia
Xenia

Popular Irish names for boys and girls

Bree

Brian

Caitlin

Connor

Eilis

Finn

Kieran

Molly

Orlaith

Ronan

 Girls' names

Habibah
(alt. Habiba)

Arabic, meaning 'beloved'.

Hadassah

Hebrew, meaning 'myrtle tree'.

Hadley

English, meaning 'heather meadow'.

Hadria

Latin, meaning 'from Adria'.

Hala

Arabic, meaning 'halo'.

Haley
(alt. Haelee, Haely, Hailee, Hailey, Hailie, Haleigh, Hali, Halie)

English, meaning 'hay meadow'.

Halima
(alt. Halina)

Arabic, meaning 'gentle'.

Hallie
(alt. Halle, Halley, Hallie)

German, meaning 'ruler of the home or estate'.

Hannah
(alt. Haana, Hana, Hanna)

Hebrew, meaning 'grace'.

Harika

Turkish, meaning 'superior one'.

Harley
(alt. Harlene)
English, meaning 'the long field'.

Harlow
English, meaning 'army hill'.

Harmony
Latin, meaning 'harmony'.

Harper
English, meaning 'minstrel'.

Harriet
(alt. Harriett, Harriette)
German, meaning 'ruler of the home or estate'.

Hattie
Shortened form of Harriet, meaning 'ruler of the home or estate'.

Haven
English, meaning 'a place of sanctuary'.

Hayden
English, meaning 'hedged valley'.

Hayley
(alt. Haylee, Hayleigh, Haylie)
English, meaning 'hay meadow'.

Hazel
(alt. Hazle)
English, from the tree of the same name.

Heather
English, from the flower of the same name.

Heaven
English, meaning 'everlasting bliss'.

Hedda
German, meaning 'warfare'.

Hedwig
German, meaning 'warfare and strife'.

Heidi
(alt. Heidy)
German, meaning 'nobility'.

Helen
(alt. Halen, Helena, Helene, Hellen)
Greek, meaning 'light'.

Helga

German, meaning 'holy and sacred'.

Helia

Greek, meaning 'sun'.

Heloise

French, meaning 'renowned in war'.

Henrietta
(alt. Henriette)

German, meaning 'ruler of the house'.

Hephzibah

Hebrew, meaning 'my delight is in her'.

Hera

Greek, meaning 'queen'. The wife of Zeus in Greek mythology.

Hermia
(alt. Hermina, Hermine, Herminia)

Greek, meaning 'messenger'.

Hermione

Greek, meaning 'earthly'. Best known for the Harry Potter character.

Hero

Greek, meaning 'brave one of the people'.

Hertha

English, meaning 'earth'.

Hesper

Greek, meaning 'evening star'.

Hester
(alt. Hestia)

Greek, meaning 'star'.

Hilary
(alt. Hillary)

Greek, meaning 'cheerful and happy'.

Hilda
(alt. Hildur)

German, meaning 'battle woman'.

Hildegarde
(alt. Hildegard)

German, meaning 'battle stronghold'.

Hildred

German, meaning 'battle counsellor'.

Hilma

German variant of Wilhelmina, meaning 'helmet'.

Hirkani

Indian, meaning 'like a diamond'.

Hollis

English, meaning 'near the holly bushes'.

Holly
(alt. Holli, Hollie)

English, from the tree of the same name.

Honey

English, meaning 'honey'.

Honor
(alt. Honour)

Latin, meaning 'woman of honour'.

Honora
(alt. Honoria)

Latin, meaning 'woman of honour'.

Hope

English, meaning 'hope'.

Hudson

English, meaning 'adventurous'.

Hortense
(alt. Hortencia, Hortensia)

Latin, meaning 'of the garden'.

Hulda

German, meaning 'loved one'.

Hyacinth

Greek, from the flower of the same name.

Girls' names

Iantha
Greek, meaning 'purple flower'.

Ichigo
Japanese, meaning 'strawberry'.

Ida
English, meaning 'prosperous'.

Idell
(alt. *Idella*)
English, meaning 'prosperous'.

Idona
Nordic, meaning 'renewal'.

Ignacia
Latin, meaning 'ardent'.

Ila
French, meaning 'island'.

Ilana
Hebrew, meaning 'tree'.

Ilaria
Italian, meaning 'cheerful'.

Ilene
American, meaning 'light'.

Iliana
(alt. *Ileana*)
Greek, meaning 'Trojan'.

Ilona
Hungarian, meaning 'light'.

Ilsa

German, meaning 'pledged to God'.

Ima

German, meaning 'embraces everything'.

Iman

Arabic, meaning 'faith'.

Imara

Hungarian, meaning 'great ruler'.

Imelda

German, meaning 'all-consuming fight'.

Imogen
(alt. Imogene)

Latin, meaning 'last-born'.

Ina

Latin, meaning 'to make feminine'.

Inaya

Arabic, meaning 'taking care'.

India
(alt. Indie)

Hindi, from the country of the same name.

Indiana

Latin, meaning 'from India'. Also a state in America.

Indigo

Greek, meaning 'deep blue dye'.

Indira
(alt. Inira)

Sanskrit, meaning 'beauty'.

Inez
(alt. Ines)

Spanish, meaning 'pure'.

Inga
(alt. Inge, Ingeborg, Inger)

Scandinavian, meaning 'guarded by Ing'.

Ingrid

Scandinavian, meaning 'beautiful'.

Io

Greek, from the mythological heroine of the same name.

Ioanna

Greek, meaning 'grace'.

Iola
(alt. Iole)

Greek, meaning 'cloud of dawn'.

Iolanthe

Greek, meaning 'violet flower'.

Iona

Greek, from the island of the same name.

Ione

Greek, meaning 'violet'.

Iorwen

Welsh, meaning 'fair'.

Iphigenia

Greek, meaning 'sacrifice'.

Ira
(alt. Iva)

Hebrew, meaning 'watchful'.

Irene
(alt. Irelyn, Irena, Irina, Irini)

Greek, meaning 'peace'.

Iris

Greek, meaning 'rainbow'. Also from the flower of the same name.

Irma

German, meaning 'universal'.

Isabel
(alt. Isabela, Isabell, Isabella, Isabelle, Isabeth, Isobel, Izabella, Izabelle)

Spanish, meaning 'pledged to God'.

Isadora

Latin, meaning 'gift of Isis'.

Ishana

Hindi, meaning 'desire'.

Isis

Egyptian, from the goddess of the same name.

Isla
(alt. Isa, Isela, Isley)

Scottish Gaelic, meaning 'river'.

Isolde

Welsh, meaning 'fair lady'.

I

Istas

Native American, meaning 'snow'.

Ivana

Slavic, meaning 'Jehovah is gracious'.

Ivette

Variation of Yvette, meaning 'yew wood'.

Ivonne

Variation of Yvonne, meaning 'yew wood'.

Ivory

Latin, meaning 'white as elephant tusks'.

Ivy

English, from the plant of the same name.

Ixia

South African, from the flower of the same name.

Boys' names for girls (female spellings)

Alex
Billie
Cori
Charlie
Elliott
Geri
Jamie
Jo
Leslie
Robyn
Toni

J Girls' names

Jaamini

Hindi, meaning 'evening'.

Jacinda
(alt. Jacinta)

Spanish, meaning 'hyacinth'.

Jackie
(alt. Jacque, Jacqui)

Shortened form of Jacqueline, meaning 'he who supplants'.

Jacqueline
(alt. Jacalyn, Jacklyn, Jaclyn, Jacquelin, Jacquelyn, Jacquline, Jaqlyn, Jaquelin, Jaqueline)

French, meaning 'he who supplants'.

Jade
(alt. Jada, Jaida, Jayda, Jayde)

Spanish, meaning 'green stone'.

Jaden
(alt. Jadyn, Jaiden, Jaidyn, Jayden)

Contraction of Jade and Hayden, meaning 'green hedged valley'.

Jael

Hebrew, meaning 'mountain goat'.

Jaime
(alt. Jaima, Jaimie, Jami, Jamie)

Spanish, meaning 'he who supplants'.

Jamila

Arabic, meaning 'lovely'.

Jan
(alt. Jann, Janna)

Hebrew, meaning 'the Lord is gracious'.

Jana
(alt. Jaana)

Hebrew, meaning 'the Lord is gracious'.

Janae
(alt. Janay)

American, meaning 'the Lord is gracious'.

Jane
(alt. Jayne)

Feminine form of the Hebrew John, meaning 'the Lord is gracious'.

Janelle
(alt. Janel, Janell, Jenelle)

American, meaning 'the Lord is gracious'.

Janet
(alt. Janette)

Scottish, meaning 'the Lord is gracious'.

Janice
(alt. Janis)

American, meaning 'the Lord is gracious'.

Janie
(alt. Janney, Jannie)

Shortened form of Janet, meaning 'the Lord is gracious'.

Janine
(alt. Janeen)

English, meaning 'the Lord is gracious'.

Janoah
(alt. Janiya, Janiyah)

Hebrew, meaning 'quiet and calm'.

January

English, meaning 'the first month'.

Jarita

Hindi-Sanskrit, meaning 'famous bird'.

Jasmine
(alt. Jasmin, Jazim, Jazmine)

Persian, meaning 'jasmine flower'.

J

Jay

Latin, meaning 'jaybird'.

Jayna

Sanskrit, meaning 'bringer of victory'.

Jean
(alt. Jeane, Jeanne)

Scottish, meaning 'the Lord is gracious'.

Jeana
(alt. Jeanna)

Latin, meaning 'queen'.

Jeanette
(alt. Jeannette, Janette)

French, meaning 'the Lord is gracious'.

Jeanie
(alt. Jeannie)

Shortened form of Jeanette, meaning 'the Lord is gracious'.

Jeanine
(alt. Jeannine)

Latin, meaning 'the Lord is gracious'.

Jemima

Hebrew, meaning 'dove'.

Jemma

Italian, meaning 'precious stone'.

Jena

Arabic, meaning 'little bird'.

Jenna

Hebrew, meaning 'the Lord is gracious'.

Jennifer
(alt. Jenifer)

Welsh, meaning 'white and smooth'.

Flower names

Acacia
Bluebell
Daisy
Flora
Hyacinth
Lilac
Petunia
Primrose
Rose
Snowdrop

Jenny
(alt. Jennie)

Shortened form of Jennifer, meaning 'white and smooth'.

Jerrie
(alt. Jeri, Jerri, Jerrie, Jerry)

German, meaning 'spear ruler'.

Jerusha

Hebrew, meaning 'married'.

Jeryl

English, meaning 'spear ruler'.

Jessa

Shortened form of Jessica, meaning 'He sees'.

Jessamy
(alt. Jessame, Jessamine, Jessamyn)

Persian, meaning 'jasmine flower'.

Jessica
(alt. Jesica, Jesika, Jessika)

Hebrew, meaning 'He sees'.

Jessie
(alt. Jesse, Jessi, Jessye)

Shortened form of Jessica, meaning 'He sees'.

Jesusa

Spanish, meaning 'mother of the Lord'.

Jethetha

Hebrew, meaning 'princess'.

Jette
(alt. Jetta, Jettie)

Danish, meaning 'black as coal'.

Jewel
(alt. Jewell)

French, meaning 'delight'.

Jezebel
(alt. Jezabel, Jezabelle)

Hebrew, meaning 'pure and virginal'. Now often used as a term for bad women.

Jill

Latin, meaning 'youthful'.

Jillian

Latin, meaning 'youthful'.

Jimena

Spanish, meaning 'heard'.

Jo

Shortened form of Joanna, meaning 'the Lord is gracious'.

Joan

Hebrew, meaning 'the Lord is gracious'.

Joanna

(alt. Joana, Joanie, Joann, Joanne, Johanna, Joni)

Hebrew, meaning 'the Lord is gracious'.

Jocasta

Italian, meaning 'lighthearted'.

Jocelyn

(alt. Jauslyn, Jocelyne, Joscelin, Joslyn)

German, meaning 'cheerful'.

Jody

(alt. Jodee, Jodi, Jodie)

Shortened form of Judith, meaning 'Jewish'.

Joelle

(alt. Joela)

Hebrew, meaning 'Jehovah is the Lord'.

Joie

French, meaning 'joy'.

Jolene

Contraction of Joanna and Darlene, meaning 'gracious darling'.

Jolie

(alt. Joely)

French, meaning 'pretty'.

Jordan

(alt. Jordana, Jordin, Jordyn)

Hebew, meaning 'descend'.

Josephine

(alt. Josefina, Josephina)

Hebrew, meaning 'Jehovah increases'.

Josie

(alt. Joss, Jossie)

Shortened form of Josephine, meaning 'Jehovah increases'.

Jovita

(alt. Jovie)

Latin, meaning 'made glad'.

Joy

Latin, meaning 'joy'.

Joyce

Latin, meaning 'joyous'.

Juanita
(alt. Juana)

Spanish, meaning 'the Lord is gracious'.

Jubilee

Hebrew, meaning 'horn of a ram'.

Judith
(alt. Judit)

Hebrew, meaning 'Jewish'.

Judy
(alt. Judi, Judie)

Shortened form of Judith, meaning 'Jewish'.

Jules

French, meaning 'Jove's child'.

Julia

Latin, meaning 'youthful'.

Julianne
(alt. Juliana, Juliann, Julianne)

Latin, meaning 'youthful'

Julie
(alt. Juli)

Shortened form of Julia, meaning 'youthful'.

Juliet
(alt. Joliet, Juliette)

Latin, meaning 'youthful'. Most often associated with Shakespeare's heroine.

June
(alt. Juna)

Latin, after the month of the same name.

Juniper

Dutch, from the shrub of the same name.

Juno
(alt. Juneau)

Latin, meaning 'queen of heaven'.

Justice

English, meaning 'to deliver what is just'.

Justine
(alt. Justina)

Latin, meaning 'fair and righteous'.

Jørgina

Dutch, meaning 'farmer'.

 Girls' names

Kadenza
(alt. Kadence)
Latin, meaning 'with rhythm'.

Kadisha
Hebrew, meaning 'religious one'.

Kaitlin
(alt. Kaitlyn)
Greek, meaning 'pure'.

Kala
(alt. Kaela, Kaiala, Kaila)
Sanskrit, meaning 'black one'.

Kali
(alt. Kailee, Kailey, Kaleigh, Kaley, Kalie, Kalli, Kally, Kaylee, Kayleigh)
Sanskrit, meaning 'black one'.

Kalila
Arabic, meaning 'beloved'.

Kalina
Slavic, meaning 'flower'.

Kalliope
Greek, from the muse of the same name.

Kallista
Greek, meaning 'most beautiful'.

Kama
Sanskrit, meaning 'love'.

Kami
Japanese, meaning 'lord'.

Place names

Adelaide
Atlanta
Brittany
Etna
Florence
India
Lydia
Madeira
Paris
Savannah

Kamilla
(alt. Kamilah)
Slavic, meaning 'serving girl'.

Kana
Hawaiian, from the demi-god of the same name.

Kandace
(alt. Kandice)
Latin, meaning 'glowing white'.

Kandy
(alt. Kandi)
Shortened form of Kandace, meaning 'glowing white'.

Kanika
African, meaning 'black cloth'.

Kara
Latin, meaning 'dear one'.

Karen
(alt. Karan, Karalyn, Karin, Karina, Karon, Karren)
Greek, meaning 'pure'.

Kari
(alt. Karie, Karri, Karrie)
Shortened form of Karen, meaning 'pure'.

Karimah
Arabic, meaning 'giving'.

Karishma
Sanskrit, meaning 'miracle'.

Karla
German, meaning 'man'.

Karly
(alt. Karlee, Karley, Karli)
German, meaning 'free man'.

Karlyn
German, meaning 'man'.

Karma
Hindi, meaning 'destiny'.

K

Karol
(alt. Karolina, Karolyn)
Slavic, meaning 'little and womanly'.

Kasey
(alt. Kacey, Kaci, Kacie, Kacy, Kasie, Kassie)
Irish Gaelic, meaning 'alert and watchful'.

Kassandra
Greek, meaning 'she who entangles men'.

Kasumi
Japanese, meaning 'of the mist'.

Katarina
(alt. Katarine, Katerina, Katharina)
Greek, meaning 'pure'.

Kate
(alt. Kat, Katie, Kathi, Kathie, Kathy, Kati, Katy)
Shortened form of Katherine, meaning 'pure'.

Katelyn
(alt. Katelin, Katelynn, Katlin, Katlyn)
Greek, meaning 'pure'.

Katherine
(alt. Katharine, Katheryn, Kathrine, Kathryn)
Greek, meaning 'pure'.

Kathleen
(alt. Kathlyn)
Greek, meaning 'pure'.

Katrina
(alt. Katina)
Greek, meaning 'pure'.

Kaveri
Indian, meaning 'sacred river'.

Kay
(alt. Kaye)
Shortened form of Katherine, meaning 'pure'.

Kayla
(alt. Kaylah)
Greek, meaning 'pure'.

Kayley
(alt. Kayley, Kayli)
American, meaning 'pure'.

Kaylin
American, meaning 'pure'.

K

Keeley
(alt. Keely)
Irish, meaning 'battle maid'.

Keila
Hebrew, meaning 'citadel'.

Keira
Irish Gaelic, meaning 'dark'.

Keisha
(alt. Keesha)
Arabic, meaning 'woman'.

Kelis
American, meaning 'beautiful'.

Kelly
(alt. Keli, Kelley, Kelli, Kellie)
Irish Gaelic, meaning 'battle maid'.

Kelsey
(alt. Kelcee, Kelcie, Kelsea, Kelsi, Kelsie)
English, meaning 'island'.

Kendall
(alt. Kendal)
English, meaning 'the valley of the River Kent'. Also a place in Cumbria.

Kendra
English, meaning 'knowing'.

Kenna
Irish Gaelic, meaning 'handsome'.

Kennedy
(alt. Kenadee, Kennedi)
Irish Gaelic, meaning 'helmet head'.

Kenya
African, from the country of the same name.

Kerensa
Cornish, meaning 'love'.

Kerrigan
Irish, meaning 'black haired'.

Kerry
(alt. Keri, Kerri, Kerrie)
Irish, from the county of the same name.

Khadijah
(alt. Khadejah)
Arabic, meaning 'premature baby'.

Kiana
(alt. Kia, Kiana)
American, meaning 'fibre'.

Kiara

Italian, meaning 'light'.

Kiki

Spanish, meaning 'home ruler'.

Kim

Shortened form of Kimberly, from the town of the same name.

Kimana

Native American, meaning 'butterfly'.

Kimberly

(alt. Kimberleigh, Kimberley)

English, from the South African town of the same name.

Kingsley

(alt. Kinsley)

English, meaning 'king's meadow'.

Kinsey

English, meaning 'king's victory'.

Kira

Greek, meaning 'lady'.

Kiri

Maori, meaning 'tree bark'.

Long names

Alexandra
Benedicta
Christabelle
Constantine
Emmanuelle
Gabrielle
Henrietta
Philomena
Rosamond
Virginia

Kirsten

(alt. Kirstin)

Scandinavian, meaning 'Christian'.

Kirstie

(alt. Kirsty)

Shortened form of Kirsten, meaning 'Christian'.

Kitty

(alt. Kittie)

Shortened form of Katherine, meaning 'pure'.

Kizzy

Hebrew, meaning 'Cassia'.

K

Klara

Hungarian, meaning 'bright'.

Komal

Hindi, meaning 'soft and tender'.

Konstantina

Latin, meaning 'steadfast'.

Kora
(alt. Kori)

Greek, meaning 'maiden'.

Kris
(alt. Krista, Kristi, Kristie, Kristy)

Shortened form of Kristen, meaning 'Christian'.

Kristen
(alt. Kristan, Kristin, Kristine, Krysten)

Greek, meaning 'Christian'.

Krystal
(alt. Kristal, Kristel)

Greek, meaning 'ice'.

Kwanza
(alt. Kwanzaa)

African, meaning 'beginning'.

Kyla
(alt. Kya, Kylah, Kyle)

Scottish, meaning 'narrow spit of land'.

Kylie
(alt. Kiley, Kylee)

Irish Gaelic, meaning 'graceful'.

Kyoko

Japanese, meaning 'girl who sees her own true image'.

Kyra

Greek, meaning 'lady'.

Kyrie

Greek, meaning 'the Lord'.

Short names

Ali
Bev
Fay
Jan
Jo
Kay
Lyn
May
Nia
Val

K

L Girls' names

Lacey
(alt. Laci, Lacie, Lacy)
French, from a nobleman's surname.

Ladonna
Italian, meaning 'lady'.

Lady
English, meaning 'bread kneader'.

Laidh
Hebrew, meaning 'lioness'.

Laila
(alt. Laelia, Layla, Leila, Lela, Lelah, Lelia)
Arabic, meaning 'night'.

Lainey
(alt. Laine, Laney)
French, meaning 'bright light'.

Lakeisha
(alt. Lakeshia)
American, meaning 'woman'.

Lakshmi
(alt. Laxmi)
Sanskrit, meaning 'good omen'. Also the Hindu goddess.

Lana
Greek, meaning 'light'.

Lani
(alt. Lanie)
Hawaiian, meaning 'sky'.

Lara
Latin, meaning 'famous'.

Laraine

French, meaning 'from Lorraine'.

Larissa

(alt. Larisa)

Greek, meaning 'lighthearted'.

Lark

(alt. Larkin)

English, meaning 'playful songbird'.

Larsen

Scandinavian, meaning 'son of Lars'.

Latifa

Arabic, meaning 'gentle and pleasant'.

Latika

Hindi, meaning 'a plant'.

Latisha

Latin, meaning 'happiness'.

Latona

(alt. Latonia)

Roman, from the mythological heroine of the same name.

Latoya

Spanish, meaning 'victorious one'.

Latrice

(alt. Latricia)

Latin, meaning 'noble'.

Laura

Latin, meaning 'laurel'.

Laurel

Latin, meaning 'laurel tree'.

Lauren

(alt. Lauran, Loren)

Latin, meaning 'laurel'.

Laveda

(alt. Lavada)

Latin, meaning 'cleansed'.

Lavender

Latin, from the plant of the same name.

Laverne

(alt. Lavern, Laverna)

Latin, from the goddess of the same name.

280

Lavinia
(alt. Lavina)

Latin, meaning 'woman of Rome'.

Lavita

American, meaning 'charming'.

Lavonne
(alt. Lavon)

French, meaning 'yew wood'.

Leah
(alt. Lea, Leia)

Hebrew, meaning 'weary'.

Leandra

Greek, meaning 'lion man'.

Leanne
(alt. Leann, Leanna, Leeann)

Contraction of Lee and Ann, meaning 'meadow grace'.

Leda

Greek, meaning 'gladness'.

Lee
(alt. Leigh)

English, meaning 'pasture or meadow'.

'Bad girl' names

Diva
Desdemona
Fifi
Lilith
Pandora
Peaches
Sadie
Scarlett
Tallulah
Xena

Leilani

Hawaiian, meaning 'flower from heaven'.

Leith

Scottish Gaelic, meaning 'broad river'.

Lena
(alt. Leena, Lina)

Latin, meaning 'light'.

Lenna
(alt. Lennie)

German, meaning 'lion's strength'.

Lenore
(alt. Lenora)

Greek, meaning 'light'.

L

Léonie
(alt. Leona, Leone)
Latin, meaning 'lion'.

Leonora
(alt. Leonor, Leonore)
Greek, meaning 'light'.

Leora
Greek, meaning 'light'.

Lerola
Latin, meaning 'like a blackbird'.

Leslie
(alt. Leslee, Lesley, Lesli)
Scottish Gaelic, meaning 'the grey castle'.

Leta
Latin, meaning 'glad and joyful'.

Letha
Greek, meaning 'forgetfulness'.

Letitia
(alt. Leticia, Lettice, Lettie)
Latin, meaning 'joy and gladness'.

Lexia
(alt. Lexi)
Greek, meaning 'defender of mankind'.

Lia
Italian, meaning 'bringer of the gospel'.

Liana
French, meaning 'to twine around'.

Libby
(alt. Libbie)
Shortened form of Elizabeth, meaning 'consecrated to God'.

Liberty
English, meaning 'freedom'.

Lida
Slavic, meaning 'loved by the people'.

Liese
(alt. Liesel, Liesl)
German, meaning 'pledged to God'.

Lila
(alt. Lilah)
Arabic, meaning 'night'.

Lilac

Latin, from the flower of the same name.

Lilia

(alt. Lilias)

Scottish, meaning 'lily'.

Lilith

Arabic, meaning 'ghost'.

Lillian

(alt. Lilian, Liliana, Lilla, Lillianna)

Latin, meaning 'lily'.

Lily

(alt. Lillie, Lilly)

Latin, from the flower of the same name.

Linda

(alt. Lynda)

Spanish, meaning 'pretty'.

Linden

(alt. Lindie, Lindy)

European, from the tree of the same name.

Lindsay

(alt. Lindsey, Linsey)

English, meaning 'island of linden trees'.

Linette

Welsh, meaning 'idol'.

Linnea

(alt. Linnae, Linny)

Scandinavian, meaning 'lime or linden tree'.

Liora

(alt. Lior)

Hebrew, meaning 'I have a light'.

Lirit

Hebrew, meaning 'musically talented'.

Lisa

(alt. Leesa, Lise, Liza)

Hebrew, meaning 'pledged to God'.

Lissa

Greek, meaning 'bee'.

Lissandra

(alt. Lisandra)

Greek, meaning 'man's defender'.

Liv

Nordic, meaning 'defence'.

Famous female singers

Annie (Lennox)
Billie (Holiday)
Dinah (Washington)
Ella (Fitzgerald)
Etta (James)
Judy (Garland)
Kate (Bush)
Kylie (Minogue)
Lily (Allen)
Nina (Simone)

Livia

Latin, meaning 'olive'.

Liz

(alt. Lizzie, Lizzy)
Shortened form of Elizabeth, meaning 'consecrated to God'.

Logan

Irish Gaelic, meaning 'small hollow'.

Lois

German, meaning 'renowned in battle'.

Lola

Spanish, meaning 'sorrows'.

Lolita

Spanish, meaning 'sorrows'.

Lona

Latin, meaning 'lion'.

Lora

Latin, meaning 'laurel'.

Lorelei

(alt. Loralai, Loralie)
German, meaning 'dangerous rock'.

Lorenza

Latin, meaning 'from Laurentium'.

Loretta

(alt. Loreto)
Latin, meaning 'laurel'.

Lori

(alt. Laurie, Lorie, Lorri)
Latin, meaning 'laurel'.

Lorna

Scottish, from the town of Lorne.

Lorraine
(alt. Loraine)

French, meaning 'from Lorraine'.

Lottie
(alt. Lotta, Lotte)

French, meaning 'little and womanly'.

Lotus

Greek, meaning 'lotus flower'.

Lou
(alt. Louie, Lue)

Shortened form of Louise, meaning 'renowned in battle'.

Louise
(alt. Louisa, Luisa)

German, meaning 'renowned in battle'.

Lourdes

French, from the town of the same name.

Love

English, meaning 'love'.

Lowri

Welsh, meaning 'crowned with laurels'.

Luanne
(alt. Luann, Luanna)

German, meaning 'renowned in battle'.

Luba

Hebrew, meaning 'dearly loved'.

Lucia
(alt. Luciana)

Italian, meaning 'light'.

Lucille
(alt. Lucile, Lucilla)

French, meaning 'light'.

Lucinda

English, meaning 'light'.

Lucretia
(alt. Lucrece)

Spanish, meaning 'light'.

Lucy
(alt. Lucie)

Latin, meaning 'light'.

Ludmilla

Slavic, meaning 'beloved of the people'.

Luella

English, meaning 'renowned in battle'.

Lulu
(alt. Lula)

German, meaning 'renowned in battle'.

Luna

Latin, meaning 'moon'.

Lupe

Spanish, from the town of the same name.

Luz

Spanish, meaning 'light'.

Lydia
(alt. Lidia)

Greek, meaning 'from Lydia'.

Lynn
(alt. Lyn, Lynne)

Spanish, meaning 'pretty'.

Lynton

English, meaning 'town of lime trees'.

Lyra

Latin, meaning 'lyre'.

Tennis players

Anna (Kournikova)

Billie Jean (King)

Justine (Henin)

Maria (Sharapova)

Monica (Seles)

Serena (Williams)

Sue (Barker)

Steffi (Graf)

Venus (Williams)

M Girls' names

Mab
Irish Gaelic, meaning 'joy'.

Mabel
(alt. Mabelle, Mable)
Latin, meaning 'loveable'.

Macaria
Spanish, meaning 'blessed'.

Machiko
Japanese, meaning 'beautiful woman'.

Macy
(alt. Macey, Maci, Macie)
French, meaning 'Matthew's estate'.

Mada
English, meaning 'from Magdala'.

Madden
(alt. Maddyn)
Irish, meaning 'little dog'.

Maddie
(alt. Maddi, Maddie, Madie)
Shortened form of Madeline, meaning 'from Magdala'.

Madeline
(alt. Madaline, Madalyn, Madeleine, Madelyn, Madelynn, Madilyn)
Greek, meaning 'from Magdala'.

Madge
Greek, meaning 'pearl'.

Madhuri
Hindi, meaning 'sweet girl'.

Madison
(alt. Maddison, Madisen, Madisyn, Madyson)
English, meaning 'son of the mighty warrior'.

Madonna
Latin, meaning 'my lady'.

Maeve
Irish Gaelic, meaning 'intoxicating'.

Mafalda
Spanish, meaning 'battle-mighty'.

Magali
Greek, meaning 'pearl'.

Magdalene
(alt. Magdalen, Magdalena)
Greek, meaning 'from Magdala'.

Maggie
Shortened form of Margaret, meaning 'pearl'.

Magnolia
Latin, from the flower of the same name.

Mahala
(alt. Mahalia)
Hebrew, meaning 'tender affection'.

Maia
(alt. Maja)
Greek, meaning 'mother'.

Maida
English, meaning 'maiden'.

Maisie
(alt. Maisey, Maisy, Maizie, Masie, Mazie)
Greek, meaning 'pearl'.

Madaio
Hawaiian, meaning 'gift from God'.

Malka
Hebrew, meaning 'queen'.

Mallory
(alt. Malorie)
French, meaning 'unhappy'.

Malvina
Gaelic, meaning 'smooth brow'.

Mamie
(alt. Mammie)

Shortened form of Margaret, meaning 'pearl'.

Mandy
(alt. Mandie)

Shortened form of Amanda, meaning 'much loved'.

Manisha

Sanskrit, meaning 'desire'.

Mansi

Hopi, meaning 'plucked flower'.

Manuela

Spanish, meaning 'the Lord is among us'.

Mara

Hebrew, meaning 'bitter'.

Marcela
(alt. Marceline, Marcella, Marcelle)

Latin, meaning 'war-like'.

Marcia

Latin, meaning 'war-like'.

Marcy
(alt. Marci, Marcie)

Latin, meaning 'war-like'.

Margaret
(alt. Margarete, Margaretta, Margarette, Margret)

Greek, meaning 'pearl'.

Margery
(alt. Marge, Margie, Margit, Margy)

French, meaning 'pearl'.

Margo
(alt. Margot)

French, meaning 'pearl'.

Marguerite
(alt. Margarita)

French, meaning 'pearl'.

Maria
(alt. Mariah)

Latin, meaning 'bitter'.

Marian
(alt. Mariam, Mariana, Marion)

French, meaning 'bitter grace'.

M

Marianne
(alt. Mariana, Mariann, Maryann, Maryanne)
French, meaning 'bitter grace'.

Maribel
American, meaning 'bitterly beautiful'.

Marie
French, meaning 'bitter'.

Mariel
(alt. Mariela, Mariella)
Dutch, meaning 'bitter'.

Marietta
(alt. Marieta)
French, meaning 'bitter'.

Marigold
English, from the flower of the same name.

Marika
Dutch, meaning 'bitter'.

Marilyn
(alt. Marilee, Marilene, Marilynn)
English, meaning 'bitter'.

Marin
American, from the county of the same name.

Marina
(alt. Marine)
Latin, meaning 'from the sea'.

Mariposa
Spanish, meaning 'butterfly'.

Maris
Latin, meaning 'of the sea'.

Marisa
Latin, meaning 'of the sea'.

Marisol
Spanish, meaning 'bitter sun'.

Marissa
American, meaning 'of the sea'.

Marjolaine
French, meaning 'marjoram'.

Marjorie
(alt. Marjory)
French, meaning 'pearl'.

Marla
Shortened form of Marlene, meaning 'bitter'.

Marlene
(alt. Marlen, Marlena)
Hebrew, meaning 'bitter'.

Marley
(alt. Marlee)
American, meaning 'bitter'.

Marlo
(alt. Marlowe)
American, meaning 'bitter'.

Marseille
French, from the city of the same name.

Marsha
English, meaning 'war-like'.

Martha
(alt. Marta)
Aramaic, meaning 'lady'.

Martina
Latin, meaning 'war-like'.

Marvel
French, meaning 'something to marvel at'.

Mary
Hebrew, meaning 'bitter'.

Masada
Hebrew, meaning 'foundation'.

Matilda
(alt. Mathilda, Mathilde, Matide)
German, meaning 'battle-mighty'.

Mattea
Hebrew, meaning 'gift of God'.

Maude
(alt. Maud)
German, meaning 'battle-mighty'.

Maura
Irish, meaning 'bitter'.

Maureen
(alt. Maurine)
Irish, meaning 'bitter'.

Mavis
French, meaning 'thrush'.

Maxine
(alt. Maxie)
Latin, meaning 'greatest'.

M

May
(alt. Mae, Maya, Maye, Mayra)
Hebrew, meaning 'gift of God'.
Also the month.

Mckenna
(alt. Mackenna)
Irish Gaelic, meaning 'son of
the handsome one'.

Mckenzie
*(alt. Mackenzie, Mckenzy,
Mikenzi)*
Irish Gaelic, meaning 'son of
the wise ruler'.

Meara
Gaelic, meaning 'filled with
happiness'.

Medea
(alt. Meda)
Greek, meaning 'ruling'.

Meg
Shortened form of Margaret,
meaning 'pearl'.

Megan
(alt. Meagan, Meghan)
Welsh, meaning 'pearl'.

Mehitabel
Hebrew, meaning 'benefited
by God'.

Mehri
Persian, meaning 'kind'.

Meiwei
Chinese, meaning 'forever
enchanting'.

Melanie
(alt. Melania, Melany, Melonie)
Greek, meaning 'dark-skinned'.

Melba
Australian, meaning 'from
Melbourne'.

Melia
(alt. Meliah)
German, meaning 'industrious'.

Melina
Greek, meaning 'honey'.

Melinda
Latin, meaning 'honey'.

Melisande
French, meaning 'bee'.

Melissa
(alt. Melisa, Mellissa)
Greek, meaning 'bee'.

Melody
(alt. Melodie)
Greek, meaning 'song'.

Melvina
Celtic, meaning 'chieftain'.

Menora
Hebrew, meaning 'candlestick'.

Mercedes
Spanish, meaning 'mercies'. Most often associated with the car.

Mercy
English, meaning 'mercy'.

Meredith
(alt. Meridith)
Welsh, meaning 'great ruler'.

Merle
French, meaning 'blackbird'.

Merry
English, meaning 'lighthearted'.

Meryl
(alt. Merrill)
Irish Gaelic, meaning 'sea-bright'.

Meta
German, meaning 'pearl'.

Mia
Italian, meaning 'mine'.

Michaela
(alt. Makaela, Makaila, Micaela, Mikaila, Mikayla)
Hebrew, meaning 'who is like the Lord'.

Michelle
(alt. Machelle, Mechelle, Michaele, Michal, Michele)
French, meaning 'who is like the Lord'.

Mickey
(alt. Mickie)
Shortened form of Michelle, meaning 'who is like the Lord'.

Mieko
Japanese, meaning 'born into wealth'.

Migdalia
Greek, meaning 'from Magdala'.

Mignon
French, meaning 'cute'.

Mika
(alt. Micah)

Hebrew, meaning 'who resembles God'.

Milada

Czech, meaning 'my love'.

Milagros

Spanish, meaning 'miracles'.

Milan

Italian, from the city of the same name.

Mildred

English, meaning 'gentle strength'.

Milena

Czech, meaning 'love and warmth'.

Miley

American, meaning 'smiley'. Made popular by Miley Cyrus.

Millicent

German, meaning 'highborn power'.

Millie
(alt. Milly)

Shortened form of Millicent, meaning 'highborn power'.

Mimi

Italian, meaning 'bitter'.

Popular song names

Alice (*All the Girls Love Alice*, Elton John)
Billie Jean (*Billie Jean*, Michael Jackson)
Caroline (*Sweet Caroline*, Neil Diamond)
Delilah (*Delilah*, Tom Jones)
Eileen (*Come on Eileen*, Dexy's Midnight Runners)
Eleanor (*Eleanor Rigby*, The Beatles)
Judy (*Judy*, The Beach Boys)
Roxanne (*Roxanne*, The Police)
Sally (*Mustang Sally*, Wilson Pickett)
Valerie (*Valerie*, Amy Winehouse & Mark Ronson)

M

Mina
(alt. Mena)
German, meaning 'love'.

Mindy
(alt. Mindi)
Latin, meaning 'honey'.

Minerva
Roman, from the goddess of the same name.

Ming
Chinese, meaning 'bright'.

Minna
German, meaning 'helmet'.

Minnie
German, meaning 'helmet'. Often associated with the Disney character Minnie Mouse.

Mira
Latin, meaning 'admirable'.

Mirabel
(alt. Mirabella, Mirabelle)
Latin, meaning 'wonderful'.

Miranda
(alt. Meranda)
Latin, meaning 'admirable'.

Mirella
(alt. Mireille, Mirela)
Latin, meaning 'admirable'.

Miriam
Hebrew, meaning 'bitter'.

Mirta
Spanish, meaning 'crown of thorns'.

Missy
Shortened form of Melissa, meaning 'bee'.

Misty
(alt. Misti)
English, meaning 'mist'.

Mitzi
German, meaning 'bitter'.

Miu
Japanese, meaning 'beautiful feather'.

Moira
(alt. Maira)
Irish, meaning 'bitter'.

M

Molly
(alt. Mollie)

American, meaning 'bitter'.

Mona

Irish Gaelic, meaning 'aristocratic'.

Monica
(alt. Monika, Monique)

Latin, meaning 'adviser'.

Montserrat
(alt. Monserrate)

Spanish, from the town of the same name.

Morag

Scottish, meaning 'star of the sea'.

Morgan
(alt. Morgann)

Welsh, meaning 'great and bright'.

Moriah

Hebrew, meaning 'the Lord is my teacher'.

Morwenna

Welsh, meaning 'maiden'.

Moselle
(alt. Mozell, Mozella, Mozelle)

Hebrew, meaning 'saviour'.

Mulan

Chinese, meaning 'wood orchid'.

Munin

Scandinavian, meaning 'good memory'.

Muriel

Irish Gaelic, meaning 'sea-bright'.

Mya
(alt. Myah)

Greek, meaning 'mother'.

Myfanwy

Welsh, meaning 'my little lovely one'.

Myra

Latin, meaning 'scented oil'.

Myrna
(alt. Mirna)

Irish Gaelic, meaning 'tender and beloved'.

Myrtle

Irish, from the shrub of the same name.

Girls' names

Nadia
(alt. Nadya)
Russian, meaning 'hope'.

Nadine
French, meaning 'hope'.

Nahara
Aramaic, meaning 'light'.

Naima
Arabic, meaning 'water nymph'.

Nakia
Egyptian, meaning 'pure'.

Nalani
Hawaiian, meaning 'serenity of the skies'.

Nan
(alt. Nanna, Nannie)
Hebrew, meaning 'grace'.

Nancy
(alt. Nanci, Nancie)
Hebrew, meaning 'grace'.

Nanette
(alt. Nannette)
French, meaning 'grace'.

Naomi
(alt. Naoma, Noemi)
Hebrew, meaning 'pleasant'.

Narcissa
Greek, meaning 'daffodil'.

Nastasia

Greek, meaning 'resurrection'.

Natalie

(alt. Natalee, Natalia, Natalya, Nathalie)

Latin, meaning 'birth day'.

Natasha

(alt. Natasa)

Russian, meaning 'birth day'.

Natividad

Spanish, meaning 'Christmas'.

Neda

English, meaning 'wealthy'.

Nedra

English, meaning 'underground'.

Neema

Swahili, meaning 'born of prosperity'.

Neka

Native American, meaning 'goose'.

Nell

(alt. Nelda, Nell, Nella, Nellie, Nelly)

Shortened form of Eleanor, meaning 'light'.

Nemi

Italian, from the lake of the same name.

Neoma

Greek, meaning 'new moon'.

Nereida

Spanish, meaning 'sea nymph'.

Nerissa

Of Greek origin, meaning 'sea nymph'.

Nettie

(alt. Neta)

Shortened form of Henrietta, meaning 'ruler of the house'.

Neva

Spanish, meaning 'snowy'.

Nevaeh

American, meaning 'heaven'.

Nhung

Vietnamese, meaning 'velvet'.

N

Niamh
(alt. Neve)
Irish, meaning 'brightness'.

Nicki
(alt. Nicky, Nikki)
Shortened form of Nicola, meaning 'victory of the people'.

Nicola
Greek, meaning 'victory of the people'.

Nicole
(alt. Nichol, Nichole, Nicolette, Nicolle, Nikole)
Greek, meaning 'victory of the people'.

Nidia
Spanish, meaning 'graceful'.

Nigella
Irish Gaelic, meaning 'champion'.

Nikita
Greek, meaning 'unconquered'.

Nila
Egyptian, meaning 'Nile'.

Nilda
German, meaning 'battle woman'.

Nimra
Arabic, meaning 'number'.

Nina
Spanish, meaning 'girl'.

Nissa
Hebrew, meaning 'sign'.

Nita
Spanish, meaning 'gracious'.

Nixie
German, meaning 'water sprite'.

Noel
(alt. Noelle)
French, meaning 'Christmas'.

Nola
Irish Gaelic, meaning 'white shoulder'.

Nona
Latin, meaning 'ninth'.

N

Nora
(alt. Norah)
Shortened form of Eleanor, meaning 'light'.

Noreen
(alt. Norine)
Irish, meaning 'light'.

Norma
Latin, meaning 'pattern'.

Normandie
(alt. Normandy)
French, from the province of the same name.

Novia
Latin, meaning 'new'.

Nuala
Irish Gaelic, meaning 'white shoulder'.

Nydia
Latin, meaning 'nest'.

Nyimbo
Swahili, meaning 'song'.

Nysa
(alt. Nyssa)
Greek, meaning 'ambition'.

Names of goddesses

Aphrodite (Love: Greek)
Ceres (Agriculture: Roman)
Eos (Dawn: Greek)
Hestia (Hearth: Greek)
Kali (Death: Indian)
Lucinda (Childbirth: Roman)
Minerva (Wisdom: Roman)
Nephthys (Death: Egyptian)
Sesheta (Stars: Egyptian)
Terra (Earth: Roman)

N

 Girls' names

Oceana
(alt. Ocean, Océane, Ocie)
Greek, meaning 'ocean'.

Octavia
Latin, meaning 'eighth'.

Oda
(alt. Odie)
Shortened form of Odessa, meaning 'long voyage'.

Odele
(alt. Odell)
English, meaning 'woad hill'.

Odelia
Hebrew, meaning 'I will praise the Lord'.

Odessa
Greek, meaning 'long voyage'.

Odette
(alt. Odetta)
French, meaning 'wealthy'.

Odile
(alt. Odilia)
French, meaning 'prospers in battle'.

Odina
Feminine form of Odin, from the Nordic god of the same name.

Odyssey
Greek, meaning 'long journey'.

Oksana
Russian, meaning 'praise to God'.

Ola
(alt. Olie)
Greek, meaning 'man's defender'.

Olena
(alt. Olene)
Russian, meaning 'light'.

Olga
Russian, meaning 'holy'.

Oliana
American, meaning 'the Lord has answered'.

Olivia
(alt. Olivev, Oliviana, Olivié)
Latin, meaning 'olive'.

Ollie
Shortened form of Olivia, meaning 'olive'.

Olwen
Welsh, meaning 'white footprint'.

Olympia
(alt. Olimpia)
Greek, meaning 'from Mount Olympus'.

Oma
(alt. Omie)
Arabic, meaning 'leader'.

Omyra
Latin, meaning 'scented oil'.

Ona
(alt. Onnie)
Shortened form of Oneida, meaning 'long awaited'.

Ondine
French, meaning 'wave of water'.

Oneida
Native American, meaning 'long awaited'.

Onyx
Latin, meaning 'veined gem'.

Oona
Irish, meaning 'unity'.

Opal

Sanskrit, meaning 'gem'.

Ophelia

(alt. Ofelia, Ophélie)

Greek, meaning 'help'. Best known from Shakespeare's play *Hamlet*.

Oprah

Hebrew, meaning 'young deer'. Most often associated with Oprah Winfrey.

Ora

Latin, meaning 'prayer'.

Orabela

Latin, meaning 'prayer'.

Colour names

Azure
Cinnabar
Ebony
Fuchsia
Ivory
Olive
Rose
Saffron
Sienna
Violet

Oralie

(alt. Oralia)

French, meaning 'golden'.

Orane

French, meaning 'rising'.

Orchid

Greek, from the flower of the same name.

Oriana

(alt. Oriane)

Latin, meaning 'dawning'.

Orla

(alt. Orlaith, Orly)

Irish Gaelic, meaning 'golden lady'.

Orlean

French, meaning 'plum'.

Ornelia

Italian, meaning 'flowering ash tree'.

Orsa

(alt. Osia, Ossie)

Latin, meaning 'bear'.

O

Otthid

Greek, meaning 'prospers in battle'.

Ottilie
(alt. Ottie)

French, meaning 'prospers in battle'.

Ouida

French, meaning 'renowned in battle'.

Oyintsa

Native American, meaning 'white duck'.

Ozette

Native American, from the village of the same name.

Popular Scottish names for boys and girls

Angus
Calum
Douglas
Elsie
Flora
Isla
Kirsty
Malcolm
Rhona
Roderick

O

P

Girls' names

Pacifica
(alt. Pacifika)

Spanish, meaning 'peaceful'.

Padma

Hindi, meaning 'lotus'.

Paige
(alt. Page)

French, meaning 'serving boy'.

Paisley

Scottish, from the town of the same name.

Palma
(alt. Palmira)

Latin, meaning 'palm tree'.

Paloma

Spanish, meaning 'dove'.

Pam

Shortened form of Pamela, meaning 'all honey'.

Pamela
(alt. Pamala, Pamella, Pamla)

Greek, meaning 'all honey'.

Pandora

Greek, meaning 'all gifted'. Also from the Greek myth.

Pangiota

Greek, meaning 'all is holy'.

Paniz

Persian, meaning 'candy'.

Pansy

French, from the flower of the same name.

Paradisa
(alt. Paradis)
Greek, meaning 'garden orchard'.

Paris
(alt. Parisa)
Greek, from the mythological hero of the same name. Also from the city.

Parker
English, meaning 'park keeper'.

Parthenia
Greek, meaning 'virginal'.

Parthenope
Greek, from the mythological Siren of the same name.

Parvati
Sanskrit, meaning 'daughter of the mountain'.

Pascale
French, meaning 'Easter'.

Pat
(alt. Patsy, Patti, Pattie, Patty)
Shortened form of Patricia, meaning 'noble'.

Patience
French, meaning 'the state of being patient'.

Patricia
(alt. Patrice)
Latin, meaning 'noble'.

Paula
Latin, meaning 'small'.

Pauline
(alt. Paulette, Paulina)
Latin, meaning 'small'.

Paxton
Latin, meaning 'peaceful town'.

Paz
Spanish, meaning 'peace'.

Pazia
Hebrew, meaning 'golden'.

Peace
English, meaning 'peace'.

Peaches
English, meaning 'peaches'.

Gem and precious stone names

Amber
Beryl
Coral
Esmerelda
Jade
Marjorie
Pearl
Ruby
Topaz

Pearl
(alt. Pearle, Pearlie, Perla)

Latin, meaning 'pale gemstone'.

Peggy
(alt. Peggie)

Greek, meaning 'pearl'.

Pelia

Hebrew, meaning 'marvel of God'.

Penelope

Greek, meaning 'bobbin worker'.

Penny
(alt. Penni, Pennie)

Greek, meaning 'bobbin worker'.

Peony

Greek, from the flower of the same name.

Perdita

Latin, meaning 'lost'.

Peri
(alt. Perri)

Hebrew, meaning 'outcome'.

Perry

French, meaning 'pear tree'.

Persephone

Greek, meaning 'bringer of destruction'.

Petra
(alt. Petrina)

Greek, meaning 'rock'.

Petula

Latin, meaning 'to seek'.

P

Petunia

Greek, from the flower of the same name.

Phaedra

Greek, meaning 'bright'.

Philippa

Greek, meaning 'horse lover'.

Philomena
(alt. Philoma)

Greek, meaning 'loved one'.

Phoebe

Greek, meaning 'shining and brilliant'.

Phoenix

Greek, meaning 'red as blood'. Also from the mythical bird.

Phyllida

Greek, meaning 'leafy bough'.

Phyllis
(alt. Phillia, Phylis)

Greek, meaning 'leafy bough'.

Pia

Latin, meaning 'pious'.

Pilar

Spanish, meaning 'pillar'.

Piera

Italian, meaning 'rock'.

Piper

English, meaning 'pipe player'.

Pippa

Shortened form of Philippa, meaning 'horse lover'.

Spelling options

C vs K (Cathy or Kathy)
E vs I (Alex or Alix)
G vs J (Georgie or Georjie)
A vs AH (Hanna or Hannah)
O vs OU (Honor or Honour)
S vs Z (Susie or Suzie)
Y vs IE (Debby or Debbie)

P

Plum

Latin, from the fruit of the same name.

Polly

Hebrew, meaning 'bitter'.

Pomona

Latin, meaning 'apple'.

Poppy

Latin, from the flower of the same name.

Portia
(alt. Porsha)

Latin, meaning 'from the Portia clan'.

Posy

English, meaning 'small flower'.

Precious

Latin, meaning 'of great worth'.

Priela

Hebrew, meaning 'fruit of God'.

Primavera

Spanish, meaning 'springtime'.

Primrose

English, meaning 'first rose'.

Princess

English, meaning 'daughter of the monarch'.

Priscilla
(alt. Prisca, Priscila)

Latin, meaning 'ancient'.

Priya

Hindi, meaning 'loved one'.

Prudence

Latin, meaning 'caution'.

Prudie

Shortened form of Prudence, meaning 'caution'.

Prunella

Latin, meaning 'small plum'.

Psyche

Greek, meaning 'breath'. Also from Greek mythology and psychological theory.

P

Names with positive meanings

Allegra – Cheerful
Augusta – Magnificent
Felicia – Lucky
Gladys – Glad
Hilary – Cheerful
Lucy – Light
Phoebe – Radiant
Rinah – Joyful
Thalia – Flourishing
Yoko – Positive

P

Girls' names

Qiana
(alt. Qianah, Qiania, Qyana, Qianne)

American, meaning 'gracious'.

Qiturah
Arabic, meaning 'incense'.

Queen
(alt. Queenie)
English, meaning 'queen'.

Quiana
American, meaning 'silky'.

Quincy
(alt. Quincey)
French, meaning 'estate of the fifth son'.

Quinn
Irish Gaelic, meaning 'counsel'.

Quintessa
Latin, meaning 'creative'.

Foreign alternatives

Emily – Emilie, Emeline
Helen – Galina, Helene
Mary – Marie, Maria, Marjan
Sarah – Sara, Sarine, Zara
Violet – Iolanthe, Yolanda

No-nickname names

Amy
Beth
Dana
Jess
Judy
June
Mia
Ruth

Q

 Girls' names

Rachel
(alt. Rachael, Rachelle)
Hebrew, meaning 'ewe'.

Radhika
Sanskrit, meaning 'prosperous'.

Rae
(alt. Ray)
Shortened form of Rachel, meaning 'ewe'.

Rafferty
Irish, meaning 'abundance'.

Rahima
Arabic, meaning 'compassionate'.

Raina
(alt. Rain, Raine, Rainey, Rayne)
Latin, meaning 'queen'.

Raissa
(alt. Raisa)
Yiddish, meaning 'rose'.

Raleigh
(alt. Rayleigh)
English, meaning 'meadow of roe deer'.

Rama
(alt. Ramey, Ramya)
Hebrew, meaning 'exalted'.

Ramona
(alt. Romona)
Spanish, meaning 'wise guardian'.

Ramsey
English, meaning 'raven island'.

Rana
(alt. Rania, Rayna)

Arabic, meaning 'beautiful thing'.

Randy
(alt. Randi)

Shortened form of Miranda, meaning 'admirable'.

Rani
Sanskrit, meaning 'queen'.

Raphaela
(alt. Rafaela, Raffaella)

Spanish, meaning 'healing God'.

Raquel
(alt. Racquel)

Hebrew, meaning 'ewe'.

Rashida
Turkish, meaning 'righteous'.

Raven
(alt. Ravyn)

English, from the bird of the same name.

Razia
Arabic, meaning 'contented'.

Reagan
(alt. Reagen, Regan)

Irish Gaelic, meaning 'descendant of Riagán'.

Reba
Shortened form of Rebecca, meaning 'joined'.

Rebecca
(alt. Rebekah)

Hebrew, meaning 'joined'.

Reese
Welsh, meaning 'fiery and zealous'.

Regina
Latin, meaning 'queen'.

Reiko
Japanese, meaning 'thankful one'.

Reina
(alt. Reyna, Rheyna)

Spanish, meaning 'queen'.

Rena
(alt. Reena)

Hebrew, meaning 'serene'.

R

Renata

Latin, meaning 'reborn'.

Rene

Greek, meaning 'peace'.

Renée
(alt. Renae)

French, meaning 'reborn'.

Renita

Latin, meaning 'resistant'.

Reshma
(alt. Resha)

Sanskrit, meaning 'silk'.

Reta
(alt. Retha, Retta)

Shortened form of Margaret, meaning 'pearl'.

Rhea

Greek, meaning 'earth'.

Rheta

Greek, meaning 'eloquent speaker'.

Rhiannon
(alt. Reanna, Reanne, Rhian, Rhianna)

Welsh, meaning 'witch'.

Rhoda

Greek, meaning 'rose'.

Rhona

Nordic, meaning 'rough island'.

Rhonda
(alt. Ronda)

Welsh, meaning 'noisy'.

Ría
(alt. Rie, Riya)

Shortened form of Victoria, meaning 'victor'.

Ricki
(alt. Rieko, Rika, Rikki)

Shortened form of Frederica, meaning 'peaceful ruler'.

Riley

Irish Gaelic, meaning 'courageous'.

Rilla

German, meaning 'small brook'.

Rima

Arabic, meaning 'antelope'.

Riona

Irish Gaelic, meaning 'like a queen'.

Ripley

English, meaning 'shouting man's meadow'.

Risa

Latin, meaning 'laughter'.

Rita

Shortened form of Margaret, meaning 'pearl'.

River
(alt. Riviera)

English, from the body of water of the same name.

Robbie
(alt. Robi, Roby)

Shortened form of Roberta, meaning 'bright flame'.

Roberta

English, meaning 'bright flame'.

Robin
(alt. Robbin, Robyn)

English, meaning 'bright flame'.

Rochelle
(alt. Richelle, Rochel)

French, meaning 'little rock'.

Rogue

French, meaning 'beggar'.

Rohina
(alt. Rohini)

Sanskrit, meaning 'sandalwood'.

Roja

Spanish, meaning 'red-haired lady'.

Roisin

Irish Gaelic, meaning 'bright flame'.

Rolanda

German, meaning 'famous land'.

Roma

Italian, meaning 'Rome'.

Romaine
(alt. Romina)

French, meaning 'from Rome'.

'Powerful' names

Adira
Edrea
Isis
Ricarda
Roxie
Ulrika

Romola
(alt. Romilda, Romily)

Latin, meaning 'Roman woman'.

Romy

Shortened form of Rosemary, meaning 'dew of the sea'.

Rona
(alt. Ronia, Ronja, Ronna)

Nordic, meaning 'rough island'.

Ronnie
(alt. Roni)

English, meaning 'strong counsel'.

Roro

Indonesian, meaning 'nobility'.

Rosa

Italian, meaning 'rose'.

Rosabel
(alt. Rosabella)

Contraction of Rose and Belle, meaning 'beautiful rose'.

Rosalie
(alt. Rosale, Rosalia, Rosalina)

French, meaning 'rose garden'.

Rosalind
(alt. Rosalinda)

Spanish, meaning 'pretty rose'.

Rosalyn
(alt. Rosaleen, Rosaline, Roselyn)

Contraction of Rose and Lynn, meaning 'pretty rose'.

Rosamond
(alt. Rosamund)

German, meaning 'renowned protector'.

Rose

Latin, from the flower of the same name.

R

Roseanne

(alt. Rosana, Rosann, Rosanna, Rosanne, Roseann, Roseanna)

Contraction of Rose and Anne, meaning 'graceful rose'.

Rosemary

(alt. Rosemarie)

Latin, meaning 'dew of the sea'.

Rosie

(alt. Rosia)

Shortened form of Rosemary, meaning 'dew of the sea'.

Rosita

Spanish, meaning 'rose'.

Rowena

(alt. Rowan)

Welsh, meaning 'slender and fair'.

Roxanne

(alt. Roxana, Roxane, Roxanna)

Persian, meaning 'dawn'.

Roxie

Shortened form of Roxanne, meaning 'dawn'.

Rubena

(alt. Rubina)

Hebrew, meaning 'behold, a son'.

Ruby

(alt. Rubi, Rubie)

English, meaning 'red gemstone'.

Rusty

American, meaning 'red-headed'.

Ruth

(alt. Ruthe, Ruthie)

Hebrew, meaning 'friend and companion'.

Popular South American names for boys and girls

Adriel

Arrian

Carolina

Coatl

Eréndira

Lily

Matlal

Rafael

Vincent

Zolin

R

 Girls' names

Saba
(alt. Sabah)
Greek, meaning 'from Sheba'.

Sabina
(alt. Sabine)
Latin, meaning 'from the Sabine tribe'.

Sabrina
Latin, meaning 'the River Severn'.

Sadella
American, meaning 'fairytale princess'.

Sadie
(alt. Sade, Sadye)
Hebrew, meaning 'princess'.

Saffron
English, from the spice of the same name.

Safiya
Arabic, meaning 'sincere friend'.

Sage
(alt. Saga, Saige)
Latin, meaning 'wise and healthy'.

Sahara
Arabic, meaning 'desert'.

Sakura
Japanese, meaning 'cherry blossom'.

Sally
(alt. Sallie)

Hebrew, meaning 'princess'.

Salome
(alt. Salma)

Hebrew, meaning 'peace'.

Sam
(alt. Sammie, Sammy)

Shortened form of Samantha, meaning 'told by God'.

Samantha

Hebrew, meaning 'told by God'.

Samara
(alt. Samaria, Samira)

Hebrew, meaning 'under God's rule'.

Sanaa

Arabic, meaning 'brilliance'.

Sandra
(alt. Saundra)

Shortened form of Alexandra, meaning 'defender of mankind'.

Sandy
(alt. Sandi)

Shortened form of Sandra, meaning 'defender of mankind'.

Sangeeta

Hindi, meaning 'musical'.

Sanna
(alt. Saniya, Sanne, Sanni)

Hebrew, meaning 'lily'.

Santana
(alt. Santina)

Spanish, meaning 'holy'.

Sapphire
(alt. Saphira)

Hebrew, meaning 'blue gemstone'.

Sarah
(alt. Sara, Sarai, Sariah)

Hebrew, meaning 'princess'.

Sasha
(alt. Sacha, Sascha)

Russian, meaning 'man's defender'.

Saskia
(alt. Saskie)

Dutch, meaning 'the Saxon people'.

Savannah
(alt. Savanah, Savanna, Savina)

Spanish, meaning 'treeless'.

Scarlett
(alt. Scarlet)

English, meaning 'scarlet'.

Scout

French, meaning 'to listen'.

Sedona
(alt. Sedna)

Spanish, from the city of the same name.

Selah
(alt Sela)

Hebrew, meaning 'cliff'.

Selby

English, meaning 'manor village'.

Selena
(alt. Salena, Salima, Salina, Selene, Selina)

Greek, meaning 'moon goddess'.

Selma

German, meaning 'Godly helmet'.

Seneca

Native American, meaning 'from the Seneca tribe'.

Sephora

Hebrew, meaning 'bird'.

September

Latin, meaning 'seventh month'.

Seraphina
(alt. Serafina, Seraphia, Seraphine)

Hebrew, meaning 'ardent'.

Serena
(alt. Sarina, Sereana)

Latin, meaning 'tranquil'.

Serenity

Latin, meaning 'serene'.

Shania
(alt. Shaina, Shana, Shaniya)

Hebrew, meaning 'beautiful'.

321

Shanice
American, meaning 'from Africa'.

Shaniqua
(alt. Shanika)
African, meaning 'warrior princess'.

Shanna
English, meaning 'old'.

Shannon
(alt. Shannan, Shanon)
Irish Gaelic, meaning 'old and ancient'.

Shantal
(alt. Shantel, Shantell)
French, meaning 'stone'.

Shanti
Hindi, meaning 'peaceful'.

Sharlene
German, meaning 'man'.

Sharon
(alt. Sharen, Sharona, Sharron, Sharyn)
Hebrew, meaning 'a plain'.

Nautical names

Coral
Halimedi
Marina
Nereida
Sagara

Shasta
American, from the mountain of the same name.

Shauna
(alt. Shawna)
Irish, meaning 'the Lord is gracious'.

Shayla
(alt. Shaylie, Shayna, Sheyla)
Irish, meaning 'blind'.

Shea
Irish Gaelic, meaning 'from the fairy fort'.

Sheena
Irish, meaning 'the Lord is gracious'.

S

Sheila
(alt. Shelia)

Irish, meaning 'blind'.

Shelby
(alt. Shelba, Shelbie)

English, meaning 'estate on the ledge'.

Shelley
(alt. Shelli, Shellie, Shelly)

English, meaning 'meadow on the ledge'.

Shenandoah

Native American, meaning 'after an Oneida chief'.

Sheridan

Irish Gaelic, meaning 'wild man'.

Sherry
(alt. Sheree, Sheri, Sherie, Sherri, Sherrie)

Shortened form of Cheryl, meaning 'man'.

Sheryl
(alt. Sherryl)

German, meaning 'man'.

Shiloh

Hebrew, from the Biblical place of the same name.

Shirley
(alt. Shirlee)

English, meaning 'bright meadow'.

Shivani

Sanskrit, meaning 'wife of Shiva'.

Shona

Irish Gaelic, meaning 'God is gracious'.

Shoshana
(alt. Shoshanna)

Hebrew, meaning 'lily'.

Shura

Russian, meaning 'man's defender'.

Sian
(alt. Sianna)

Welsh, meaning 'the Lord is gracious'.

S

Sibyl
(alt. Sybil)

Greek, meaning 'seer and oracle'.

Siffhi

Hindi, meaning 'spiritual powers'.

Sidney
(alt. Sydney)

English, meaning 'from St Denis'.

Sidonie
(alt. Sidonia, Sidony)

Latin, meaning 'from Sidonia'.

Siena
(alt. Sienna)

Latin, from the town of the same name.

Sierra

Spanish, meaning 'saw'.

Signa
(alt. Signe)

Scandinavian, meaning 'victory'.

Sigrid

Nordic, meaning 'fair victory'.

Silja

Scandinavian, meaning 'blind'.

Simcha

Hebrew, meaning 'joy'.

Simone
(alt. Simona)

Hebrew, meaning 'listening intently'.

Sinead

Irish, meaning 'the Lord is gracious'.

Siobhan

Irish, meaning 'the Lord is gracious'.

Siren
(alt. Sirena)

Greek, meaning 'entangler'.

Siria

Spanish, meaning 'glowing'.

Sisika

Native American, meaning 'like a bird'.

S

Skye
(alt. Sky)

Scottish, from the island of the same name.

Skyler
(alt. Skyla, Skylar)

Dutch, meaning 'giving shelter'.

Sloane
(alt. Sloan)

Irish Gaelic, meaning 'man of arms'.

Socorro

Spanish, meaning 'to aid'.

Sojourner

English, meaning 'temporary stay'.

Solana

Spanish, meaning 'sunlight'.

Solange

French, meaning 'with dignity'.

Soledad

Spanish, meaning 'solitude'.

Soleil

French, meaning 'sun'.

Solveig

Scandinavian, meaning 'woman of the house'.

Sona

Arabic, meaning 'golden one'.

Sonia
(alt. Sonja, Sonya)

Greek, meaning 'wisdom'.

Sophia
(alt. Sofia, Sofie, Sophie)

Greek, meaning 'wisdom'.

Sophronia

Greek, meaning 'sensible'.

Soraya

Persian, meaning 'princess'.

Sorcha

Irish Gaelic, meaning 'bright and shining'.

Sorrel

English, from the herb of the same name.

Stacey
(alt. Stacie, Stacy)

Greek, meaning 'resurrection'.

Star
(alt. Starla, Starr)
English, meaning 'star'.

Stella
Latin, meaning 'star'.

Stephanie
(alt. Stefanie, Stephani, Stephania, Stephany)
Greek, meaning 'crowned'.

Sue
(alt. Susie, Suzy)
Shortened form of Susan, meaning 'lily'.

Sukey
(alt. Sukey, Sukie)
Shortened form of Susan, meaning 'lily'.

Summer
English, from the season of the same name.

Sunday
English, meaning 'the first day'.

Sunny
(alt. Sun)
English, meaning 'of a pleasant temperament'.

Suri
Persian, meaning 'red rose'.

Surya
Hindi, from the god of the same name.

Susan
(alt. Susann, Suzan)
Hebrew, meaning 'lily'.

Susannah
(alt. Susana, Susanna, Susanne, Suzanna, Suzanne)
Hebrew, meaning 'lily'.

Svea
Swedish, meaning 'of the motherland'.

Svetlana
Russian, meaning 'star'.

Swanhild
Saxon, meaning 'battle swan'.

Sylvia
(alt. Silvia, Sylvie)
Latin, meaning 'from the forest'.

T

Girls' names

Tabitha
(alt. Tabatha)
Aramaic, meaning 'gazelle'.

Tahira
Arabic, meaning 'virginal'.

Tai
Chinese, meaning 'big'.

Taima
(alt. Taina)
Native American, meaning 'peal of thunder'.

Tajsa
Polish, meaning 'princess'.

Talia
(alt. Tali)
Hebrew, meaning 'heaven's dew'.

Taliesin
Welsh, meaning 'shining brow'.

Talise
(alt. Talyse)
Native American, meaning 'lovely water'.

Talitha
Aramaic, meaning 'young girl'.

Tallulah
(alt. Taliyah)
Native American, meaning 'leaping water'.

Tamara
(alt. Tamera)
Hebrew, meaning 'palm tree'.

Famous artists

Barbara (Hepworth)
Bridget (Riley)
Louise (Bourgeois)
Tracey (Emin)
Yoko (Ono)

Tamatha
(alt. Tametha)

American, meaning 'dear Tammy'.

Tamika
(alt. Tameka)

American, meaning 'people'.

Tammy
(alt. Tami, Tammie)

Shortened form of Tamsin, meaning 'twin'.

Tamsin

Hebrew, meaning 'twin'.

Tanis

Spanish, meaning 'to make famous'.

Tanya
(alt. Tania, Tanya, Tonya)

Shortened form of Tatiana, meaning 'from the Tatius clan'.

Tao

Chinese, meaning 'like a peach'.

Tara
(alt. Tarah, Tera)

Irish Gaelic, meaning 'rocky hill'.

Tasha
(alt. Taisha, Tarsha)

Shortened form of Natasha, meaning 'Christmas'.

Tatiana
(alt. Tayana)

Russian, meaning 'from the Tatius clan'.

Tatum

English, meaning 'light-hearted'.

Tawny
(alt. Tawanaa, Tawnee, Tawnya)

English, meaning 'golden brown'.

T

Taya

Greek, meaning 'poor one'.

Taylor

(alt. Tayler)

English, meaning 'tailor'.

Tea

Greek, meaning 'goddess'.

Teagan

(alt. Teague, Tegan)

Irish Gaelic, meaning 'poet'.

Teal

English, from the bird of the same name.

Tecla

Greek, meaning 'fame of God'.

Tehile

Hebrew, meaning 'song of praise'.

Temperance

English, meaning 'virtue'.

Tempest

French, meaning 'storm'.

Teresa

(alt. Terese, Tereza, Theresa, Therese)

Greek, meaning 'harvest'.

Terry

(alt. Teri, Terrie)

Shortened form of Teresa, meaning 'harvest'.

Tessa

(alt. Tess, Tessie)

Shortened form of Teresa, meaning 'harvest'.

Thais

Greek, from the mythological heroine of the same name.

Thalia

Greek, meaning 'blooming'.

Thandi

(alt. Thana)

Arabic, meaning 'thanksgiving'.

Thea

Greek, meaning 'goddess'.

Theda

German, meaning 'people'.

Thelma

Greek, meaning 'will'.

Theodora

Greek, meaning 'gift of God'.

Theodosia

Greek, meaning 'gift of God'.

Thisbe

Greek, from the mythological heroine of the same name.

Thomasina

(alt. Thomasin, Thomasine, Thomasyn)

Greek, meaning 'twin'.

Thora

Scandinavian, meaning 'Thor's struggle'.

Tia

(alt. Tiana)

Spanish, meaning 'aunt'.

Tiara

Latin, meaning 'jewelled headband'.

Tien

Vietnamese, meaning 'fairy child'.

Tierney

Irish Gaelic, meaning 'Lord'.

Tierra

(alt. Tiera)

Spanish, meaning 'land'.

Tiffany

(alt. Tiffani, Tiffanie)

Greek, meaning 'God's appearance'.

Tiggy

Shortened form of Tigris, meaning 'tiger'.

Tigris

Irish Gaelic, meaning 'tiger'.

Tilda

Shortened form of Matilda, meaning 'battle-mighty'.

Tillie

(alt. Tilly)

Shortened form of Matilda, meaning 'battle-mighty'.

Timothea

Greek, meaning 'honouring God'.

Tina
(alt. Teena, Tena)

Shortened form of Christina, meaning 'anointed Christian'.

Tirion

Welsh, meaning 'kind and gentle'.

Tirzah

Hebrew, meaning 'pleasantness'.

Titania

Greek, meaning 'giant'.

Toby
(alt. Tobi)

Hebrew, meaning 'God is good'.

Tomoko

Japanese, meaning 'intelligent'.

Toni
(alt. Tony)

Latin, meaning 'invaluable'.

Tonia
(alt. Tonja, Tonya)

Russian, meaning 'praiseworthy'.

Topaz

Latin, meaning 'golden gemstone'.

Tori
(alt. Tora)

Shortened form of Victoria, meaning 'victory'.

Tova
(alt. Tovah, Tove)

Hebrew, meaning 'good'.

Tracy
(alt. Tracey, Tracie)

Greek, meaning 'harvest'.

Treva

Welsh, meaning 'homestead'.

Tricia

Shortened form of Patricia, meaning 'aristocratic'.

Autumn names

Aeria
Axelle
Peace
Shanti
Zulma

331

Trilby

English, meaning 'vocal trills'.
Also a kind of hat.

Trina

(alt. Trena)

Greek, meaning 'pure'.

Trinity

Latin, meaning 'triad'.

Trisha

Shortened form of Patricia, meaning 'noble'.

Trista

Latin, meaning 'sad'.

Trixie

Shortened form of Beatrix, meaning 'bringer of gladness'.

Trudy

(alt. Tru, Trudie)

Shortened form of Gertrude, meaning 'strength of a spear'.

Tullia

Spanish, meaning 'bound for glory'.

Tunder

Hungarian, meaning 'fairy'.

Twyla

(alt. Twila)

American, meaning 'star'.

Tyler

English, meaning 'tiler'.

Tyra

Scandinavian, meaning 'Thor's struggle'.

Tzipporah

Hebrew, meaning 'bird'.

Popular Spanish names for boys and girls

Alegra
Alonto
Carlos
Carmen
Fernando
Jorge
Latoya
Mirta
Pablo
Yolanda

Girls' names

Udaya

Indian, meaning 'dawn'.

Ula
(alt. Ulla)

Celtic, meaning 'gem of the sea'.

Ulrika
(alt. Urica)

German, meaning 'power of the wolf'.

Uma

Sanskrit, meaning 'flax'.

Una

Latin, meaning 'one'.

Undine

Latin, meaning 'little wave'.

Famous athletes

Denise (Lewis)
Kelly (Holmes)
Mary (Rand)
Paula (Radcliffe)
Sally (Gunnell)

Unice

Greek, meaning ' victorious'.

Unique

Latin, meaning 'only one'.

Unity

English, meaning 'oneness'.

Uriela

Hebrew, meaning 'God's light'.

Urja
(alt. Urjitha)

Indian, meaning 'energy'.

Ursula

Latin, meaning 'little female bear'.

Uta

German, meaning 'prospers in battle'.

V

Girls' names

Vada
German, meaning 'famous ruler'.

Valdis
(alt. Valdiss, Valdys, Valdyss)
Norse, meaning 'goddess of the dead', based on the mythological goddess of the same name.

Vale
Shortened form of Valencia, meaning 'strong and healthy'.

Valencia
(alt. Valancy, Valarece)
Latin, meaning 'strong and healthy'.

Valentina
Latin, meaning 'strong and healthy'.

Valentine
Latin, from the saint of the same name.

Valeria
Latin, meaning 'to be healthy and strong'.

Valerie
(alt. Valarie, Valery, Valorie)
Latin, meaning 'to be healthy and strong'.

Valia
(alt. Vallie)
Shortened form of Valerie, meaning 'to be healthy and strong'.

Vandana
Sanskrit, meaning 'worship'.

Vanessa
(alt. Vanesa)
English, from the *Gulliver's Travels* character of the same name.

Vanetta
(alt. Vanettah, Vaneta, Vanete, Vanity)
Greek, alternative of Vanessa, meaning 'like a butterfly'.

Vanity
Latin, meaning 'self-obsessed'.

Vashti
Persian, meaning 'beauty'.

Veda
Sanskrit, meaning 'knowledge and wisdom'.

Vega
Arabic, meaning 'falling vulture'.

Velda
German, meaning 'ruler'.

Vella
American, meaning 'beautiful'.

Velma
English, meaning 'determined protector'.

Venice
(alt. Venetia, Venita)
Latin, from the city of the same name.

Venus
Latin, from the Roman goddess of the same name.

Vera
(alt. Verla, Verlie)
Slavic, meaning 'faith'.

Verda
(alt. Verdie)
Latin, meaning 'spring-like'.

Christmas names

Holly
Ivy
Mary
Natalie
Robyn

Verena

Latin, meaning 'true'.

Verity

Latin, meaning 'truth'.

Verna

(alt. Vernie)

Latin, meaning 'spring green'.

Verona

Latin, from the city of the same name.

Veronica

(alt. Verica, Veronique)

Latin, meaning 'true image'.

Veruca

Latin, meaning 'wart'.

Vesta

Latin, from the Roman goddess of the same name.

Vevina

Scottish, meaning 'pleasant lady'.

Vicenta

Latin, meaning 'prevailing'.

Vicky

(alt. Vicki, Vickie, Vikki, Vix)

Shortened form of Victoria, meaning 'victory'.

Victoria

Latin, meaning 'victory'.

Vida

Spanish, meaning 'life'.

Vidya

Sanskrit, meaning 'knowledge'.

Vienna

Latin, from the city of the same name.

Vigdis

Scandinavian, meaning 'war goddess'.

Vina
(alt. Vena)
Spanish, meaning 'vineyard'.

Viola
Latin, meaning 'violet'.

Violet
(alt. Violetta)
Latin, meaning 'purple'.

Virgie
Shortened form of Virginia, meaning 'maiden'.

Virginia
(alt. Virginie)
Latin, meaning 'maiden'.

Visara
Sanskrit, meaning 'celestial'.

Vita
Latin, meaning 'life'.

Vittoria
Variation of Victoria, meaning 'victory'.

Viva
Latin, meaning 'alive'.

Viveca
Scandinavian, meaning 'war fortress'.

Vivian
(alt. Vivien, Vivienne)
Latin, meaning 'lively'.

Vonda
Czech, meaning 'from the tribe of Vandals'.

Food and drinks-inspired names

Anise
Brandy
Cinnamon
Coco
Ginger
Madeleine
Olive
Polenta
Saffron

V

Girls' names

Waleska
Polish, meaning 'beautiful'.

Wallis
English, meaning 'from Wales'.

Walta
African, meaning 'like a shield'.

Wanda
(alt. Waneta, Wanita)
Slavic, meaning 'tribe of the vandals'.

Waneta
(alt. Wanita)
Variation of Wanda, meaning 'tribe of the vandals'.

Wanita
Variation of Wanda meaning 'tribe of the vandals'.

Wava
English, meaning 'way'.

Waverly
Old English, meaning 'meadow of aspens'.

Wendy
English, meaning 'friend'.

Wharton
English, meaning 'from the river'.

Whisper
English, meaning 'whisper'.

Whitley
Old English, meaning 'white meadow'.

Whitney

Old English, meaning 'white island'.

Wilda

German, meaning 'willow tree'.

Wilfreda

English feminine form of Wilfred, meaning 'to will peace'.

Wilhelmina

German, meaning 'helmet'.

Willene
(alt. Willia)

German, meaning 'helmet'.

Willow

English, from the tree of the same name.

Wilma

German, meaning 'protection'.

Winifred

Old English, meaning 'holy and blessed'.

Winnie

Shortened form of Winifred, meaning 'holy and blessed'.

Winona
(alt. Wynona)

Indian, meaning 'first born daughter'.

Winslow

English, meaning 'friend's hill'.

Winter

English, meaning 'winter'.

Wisteria

English, meaning 'flower'.

Wren

English, from the bird of the same name.

Wynda

Scottish, meaning 'of the narrow passage'.

Wynne

Welsh, meaning 'white'.

Bird names

Avis
Evelyn
Raven
Starling
Teal

W

Girls' names

Xanadu
African, meaning 'of exotic paradise'.

Xanthe
(alt. Xanthe)
Greek, meaning 'blonde'.

Xanthippe
Greek, meaning 'nagging'.

Xaverie
Greek, meaning 'bright'.

Xaviera
Arabic, meaning 'bright'.

Xena
Greek, meaning 'foreigner'.

Xenia
Greek, meaning 'foreigner'.

Ximena
Greek, meaning 'listening'.

Xiomara
Spanish, meaning 'battle-ready'.

Xiu
Chinese, meaning 'elegant'.

Xochitl
Spanish, meaning 'flower'.

Xoey
Variant of Zoe, meaning 'life'.

Xristina

Variation of Christina, meaning 'follower of Christ'.

Xylia

(alt. Xylina, Xyloma)

Greek, meaning 'from the woods'.

Popular Welsh names for boys and girls

Aeron

Bryn

Dylan

Elen

Guinevere

Myfanwy

Owain

Rhys

Wallace

Wynne

Y Girls' names

Yadira
Arabic, meaning 'worthy'.

Yael
Hebrew, meaning 'mountain goat'.

Yaffa
(alt. Yahaira, Yajaira)
Hebrew, meaning 'lovely'.

Yanha
Arabic, meaning 'dovelike'.

Yamilet
Arabic, meaning 'beautiful'.

Yana
Hebrew, meaning 'the Lord is gracious'.

Yanira
Hawaiian, meaning 'pretty'.

Yareli
Latin, meaning 'golden'.

Yaretzi
(alt. Yaritza)
Hawaiian, meaning 'forever beloved'.

Yasmin
(alt. Yasmeen, Yasmina)
Persian, meaning 'jasmine flower'.

Yelena
Greek, meaning 'bright and chosen'.

Yeraldina
Spanish, meaning 'ruled with a spear'.

Yesenia
Arabic, meaning 'flower'.

Yetta
English, from Henrietta, meaning 'ruler of the house'.

Yeva
Hebrew variant of Eve, meaning 'life'.

Ylva
Old Norse, meaning 'sea wolf'.

Yoki
(alt. Yoko)
Native American, meaning 'rain'.

Yolanda
(alt. Yolonda)
Spanish, meaning 'violet flower'.

Yoselin
English, meaning 'lovely'.

Yoshiko
Japanese, meaning 'good child'.

Fiery names

Ardea
Blaise
Enya
Vesta

Yovela
Hebrew, meaning 'jubilee'.

Ysabel
English, meaning 'God's promise'.

Ysanne
Contraction of Isabel and Anne.

Yuki
Japanese, meaning 'lucky'.

Yuliana
Latin, meaning 'youthful'.

Yuridia
Russian, meaning 'farmer'.

Yusia
Arabic, meaning 'success'.

Yvette
(alt. Yvonne)
French, meaning 'yew'.

Z Girls' names

Zafira
Arabic, meaning 'successful'.

Zahara
(alt. Zahava, Zahra)
Arabic, meaning 'flowering and shining'.

Zaida
(alt. Zaide)
Arabic, meaning 'prosperous'.

Zalika
Swahili, meaning 'well born'.

Zaltana
Arabic, meaning 'high mountain'.

Zamia
Greek, meaning 'pine cone'.

Zaneta
(alt. Zanceta, Zanetah, Zanett, Zanetta)
Hebrew, meaning 'a gracious present from God'.

Zaniyah
Arabic, meaning 'lily'.

Zara
(alt. Zaria, Zariah, Zora)
Arabic, meaning 'radiance'.

Zelda
German, meaning 'dark battle'.

Zelia
(alt. Zella)
Scandinavian, meaning 'sunshine'.

Zelma

German, meaning 'helmet'.

Zemirah

Hebrew, meaning 'joyous melody'.

Zena

(alt. Zenia, Zina)

Greek, meaning 'hospitable'.

Zenaida

Greek, meaning 'the life of Zeus'.

Zenobia

Latin, meaning 'the life of Zeus'.

Zephyr

Greek, meaning 'the west wind'.

Zetta

Italian, meaning 'Z'.

Zia

Arabic, meaning 'light and splendour'.

Zinaida

Greek, meaning 'belonging to Zeus'.

Zinnia

Latin, meaning 'flower'.

Zipporah

Hebrew, meaning 'bird'.

Zita

(alt. Ziva)

Spanish, meaning 'little girl'.

Zoe

Greek, meaning 'life'.

Zoila

Greek, meaning 'life'.

Zorina

Slavic, meaning 'golden'.

Zoraida

Spanish, meaning 'captivating woman'.

Zosia

(alt. Zosima)

Greek, meaning 'wisdom'.

Zoya

Greek, meaning 'life'.

Zula

African, meaning 'brilliant'.

Zuleika

Arabic, meaning 'fair and intelligent'.

Zulma

Arabic, meaning 'peace'.

Zuzana

Hebrew, meaning 'lily'.

Zuzu

Czech, meaning 'flower'.

Z